MODERN WORLD NATIONS

AFGHANISTAN

ARGENTINA

AUSTRALIA

AUSTRIA

BAHRAIN

BANGLADESH

BELGIUM

BERMUDA

BOLIVIA

BOSNIA AND
  HERZEGOVINA

BRAZIL

CANADA

CHILE

CHINA

COLOMBIA

COSTA RICA

CROATIA

CUBA

DEMOCRATIC REPUBLIC
  OF THE CONGO

THE DOMINICAN
  REPUBLIC

EGYPT

ENGLAND

ETHIOPIA

FINLAND

FRANCE

REPUBLIC OF GEORGIA

GERMANY

GHANA

GREECE

GUATEMALA

HONDURAS

ICELAND

INDIA

INDONESIA

IRAN

IRAQ

IRELAND

ISRAEL

ITALY

JAMAICA

JAPAN

KAZAKHSTAN

KENYA

KUWAIT

MEXICO

NEPAL

THE NETHERLANDS

NEW ZEALAND

NICARAGUA

NIGERIA

NORTH KOREA

NORWAY

PAKISTAN

PANAMA

PERU

THE PHILIPPINES

POLAND

PORTUGAL

PUERTO RICO

RUSSIA

RWANDA

SAUDI ARABIA

SCOTLAND

SENEGAL

SOUTH AFRICA

SOUTH KOREA

SPAIN

SWEDEN

SYRIA

TAIWAN

THAILAND

TURKEY

UKRAINE

THE UNITED STATES

UZBEKISTAN

VENEZUELA

VIETNAM

Nicaragua

Charles F. Gritzner

An imprint of Infobase Publishing

Frontispiece: Flag of Nicaragua

Cover: An active volcano looms over rich, fertile fields on Isla de Ometepe, Nicaragua

Nicaragua

Copyright © 2010 by Infobase Publishing

Chelsea House
An imprint of Infobase Publishing
132 West 31st Street
New York NY 10001

Library of Congress Cataloging-in-Publication Data
Gritzner, Charles F.
  Nicaragua / Charles F. Gritzner.
      p. cm. — (Modern world nations)
  Includes bibliographical references and index.
  ISBN 978-1-60413-619-7 (hardcover)
  1. Nicaragua—Juvenile literature. I. Title. II. Series.

  F1523.2.G76 2010
  972.85--dc22
                                    2009049801

Chelsea House books are available at special discounts when purchased in bulk quantities for businesses, associations, institutions, or sales promotions. Please call our Special Sales Department in New York at (212) 967-8800 or (800) 322-8755.

You can find Chelsea House on the World Wide Web at
http://www.chelseahouse.com

Text design by Takeshi Takahashi
Cover design by Alicia Post
Composition by EJB Publishing Services
Cover printed by Yurchak Printing, Landisville, Pa.
Book printed and bound by Yurchak Printing, Landisville, Pa.
Printed in the United States of America

This book is printed on acid-free paper.

All links and Web addresses were checked and verified to be correct at the time of publication. Because of the dynamic nature of the Web, some addresses and links may have changed since publication and may no longer be valid.

Table of Contents

Nicaragua

1

Introducing Nicaragua

Welcome to Nicaragua, the largest country in Central America. You are about to launch a reading journey through this fascinating nation that occupies a portion of the narrow land corridor (isthmus) that joins Mexico and South America. Before we begin the trip, we need to know where we are traveling.

Nicaragua is one of seven countries within Central America. This region extends from the border between Guatemala and Belize southward to the boundary between Panama and the South American continent. Nicaragua and its Central American neighbors are often referred to as the "Banana Republics." The nickname comes from an earlier era during which the region produced much of the world's commercial supply of the tasty fruit. Central America also is part of a larger geographic region—Middle America. This area includes Mexico, the Central American Republics, and the islands of the Caribbean.

For thousands of years before the Spaniards arrived in the fifteenth century, Central America was home to various groups of indigenous peoples. Nicaragua was no exception. Some controversy exists in regard to the origin of the name "Nicaragua," but it is almost certain that it is at least partially of Native origin. When Spaniards arrived in the western part of present-day Nicaragua, they found the Nicaraocali tribe living on the shores of huge Lake Cocibolca (today's Lake Nicaragua). The tribe's chief was named Nicarao. *Agua* is the Spanish word for water. It seems likely that the chief's name, Nicarao, was combined with agua, to create the name of both the country and its largest body of water, Lake Nicaragua.

Nicaragua shares a common Spanish heritage with about 20 other lands and peoples located south of the U.S.-Mexico border (including several Caribbean countries such as Cuba, Puerto Rico, and the Dominican Republic). Nicaragua has two immediate neighbors. To the north lies the often troubled and turbulent Honduras. To the south, Nicaragua is bordered by relatively stable and prosperous Costa Rica. The North Pacific Ocean bathes its western shores. Its eastern border is formed by the Caribbean Sea (a branch of the North Atlantic Ocean).

In terms of its physical geography, Nicaragua is a tropical land. Its northernmost point reaches to about 15° North Latitude, thereby placing the entire country well within the tropics. Temperatures remain high throughout the year and experience little variation from season to season. Cool conditions are experienced only in the country's Central Highlands. Rainfall is abundant in most locations, although much of the country experiences wet "summer" and drier "winter" seasons.

Nicaragua's terrain varies from almost table-flat coastal plains to rugged highlands. Lush tropical rain forests blanket much of Nicaragua's soggy eastern lowland plains. This remote area continues to be the homeland of many indigenous peoples. Otherwise, it supports little economic activity and has few towns or, for that matter, roads. Much of the interior is

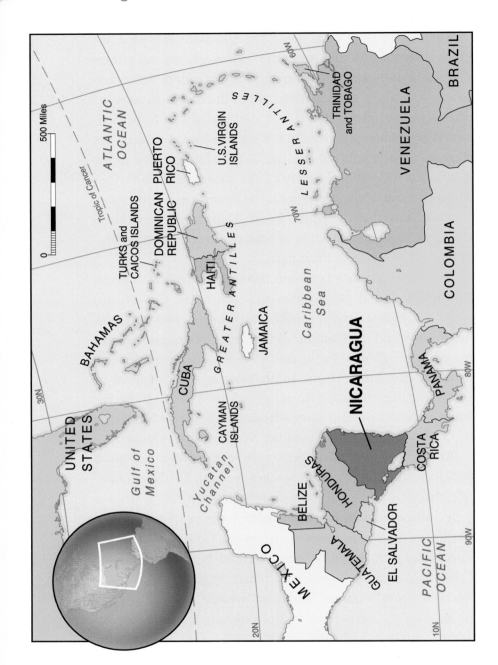

Nicaragua, the largest country in Central America, is bordered by the Caribbean Sea to the east, the North Pacific Ocean to the west, Honduras to the north, and Costa Rica to the south. The country covers an area of 50,336 square miles (130,370 square kilometers), which is about the size of New York State.

mountainous. The advantage of cooler temperatures is offset by rugged terrain, limited access, and scant economic activity. Despite its seemingly more comfortable weather conditions, few Nicaraguans live in this part of their country.

Most of the country's 5.9 million people live in the Western Lowlands that cover about one-quarter of its total area. Here are the major cities, including the country's capital and largest urban center, Managua, home to an estimated 1.4 million residents. The region is home to the largest lake in Central America and the second biggest in all of Latin America, Lake Nicaragua.

Unfortunately for Nicaraguans, their country experiences some of the deadliest natural disasters. Hurricanes have struck the country on numerous occasions, often with catastrophic winds, rain, and coastal surges of wind-driven seawater. Earthquakes have shaken the country to its very foundation on numerous occasions. Most communities—particularly in the west, including Managua—have been leveled on more than one occasion. The land is studded with about 20 active volcanoes, some of which angrily belch lava, ash, steam, and gasses with considerable regularity.

Nicaragua is also home to some dangerous wildlife. In the steaming tropical weather, do you feel like cooling off with a swim in Lake Nicaragua? Be careful: It is one of the only freshwater lakes in the world that is home to sharks! And, of course, you never know whether a hungry piranha may be waiting in the murky water, ready to strike!

History has been both kind and cruel to Nicaragua. It has blessed the country with many opportunities, including an abundance of natural resources. Rich deposits of gold first lured Spaniards to this tropical land. According to some studies, Christopher Columbus came ashore here during his fourth voyage in 1502. At the time, he marveled at the gold jewelry worn by Native peoples. (In fact, as you will learn in Chapter 3, it is entirely possible that the name "America" had its origin in Nicaragua.) Attracted by the region's potential wealth, the

Lake Nicaragua, Central America's largest freshwater lake, is home to the world's only freshwater sharks. Ometepe Island was formed by the volcanoes Concepcíon and Maderas (*background*) and has a population of 42,000.

Spaniards established a settlement, Granada, on the northwest shore of Lake Nicaragua in 1524. It is the oldest continuously inhabited Spanish colonial city on the American mainland. (Panama City, Panama, was founded in 1519, but it was later destroyed and rebuilt at a new location about 5 miles [8 kilometers] from the original site.)

Nicaragua was occupied by Native peoples when Europeans arrived, as was true of all other countries within the

Americas. Sadly, Nicaragua's indigenous population suffered the same dire fate as did nearly all other Amerindians. Europeans introduced diseases against which Native peoples had no immunity. Additionally, warfare, hunger, and other hardships brought about a rapid and almost complete reduction in Native populations.

Politically, Nicaragua has been in turmoil throughout much of its history. Constitutions have come and gone, as have leaders, the latter often by assassination or other forceful removal. During the twentieth century, the country suffered under a stifling dictatorship that lasted four decades. During the period of tight dictatorial rule by the Somoza family, a small power-elite enjoyed unimaginable prosperity. Most citizens, however, experienced the dual pains of powerlessness and poverty. No sooner had this period ended than the country was torn apart by a bitter decade-long civil war.

Even today, Nicaragua suffers the consequences of its long and relatively recent period of political instability. The country's economy, for example, is the second poorest in the Americas on a per capita basis. Only Haiti is poorer. Living conditions in Nicaragua are slowly improving, but they have a long way to go before Nicaraguans enjoy living conditions comparable to others within even the same relatively poor region.

Nicaragua offers some surprises in terms of its human geography. For example, its population density is the lowest among the Spanish-speaking countries of Central America. There is plenty of room for settlement to expand. And most Nicaraguans, almost 7 of every 10 of them, are *mestizos*, people of mixed Amerindian and white European ancestry. There are also many blacks, Amerindians, Asians, and others who contribute to the country's rich diversity of people.

For a Latin American country, Nicaragua has a surprisingly low percentage of Roman Catholics in its population. In this category, it ranks lower than any other Spanish- (or

Portuguese-) speaking country in Latin America. About 25 percent of the population belongs to a Protestant faith. There are a number of Protestant denominations in Nicaragua that claim rather large followings.

Politically, Nicaraguans take pride in the fact that their country was the very first in Latin America to elect a woman to the presidency. Violeta Chamorro was elected to the country's highest office in 1990.

This book takes you on a journey through Nicaragua's varied physical landscapes and exposes you to its numerous environmental hazards. You then will travel back through corridors of time to see how historical events have helped mold Nicaragua's current social, political, and economic conditions. Returning to the present, you will visit with the Nicaraguan people and learn about their population, settlement, ethnicity, and culture. Then, moving along, you may be shocked at the country's seemingly chronic inability to govern itself effectively. You then will visit the country's farms, factories, businesses, and other economic activities in order to learn how the people make a living. Our journey would not be complete without visiting with Nicaraguans to see how they are living today. Finally, as your trip ends, you will glimpse into the future to see what it holds in store for the Nicaraguan people. Are you ready to start your journey? Be sure to bring along some sunscreen and insect repellent!

2

Physical Landscapes

Nicaragua is often called "the land of lakes and volcanoes." In this chapter, you will experience the country's environmental diversity as you visit its varied conditions and regions. We will begin with a brief explanation of major conditions. This will be followed by a glimpse of the country's three major physical regions, including land, weather, plant and animal life, and other important features. In order to understand Nicaragua's natural environmental conditions, one must place the country in the big picture of global influences. After all, many places around the world experience physical conditions similar to those of this Central American country. Let's see how things tie together.

TERRAIN

The land occupied by Nicaragua did not even exist until about 20 million years ago. Perhaps you have heard of plate tectonics—that huge

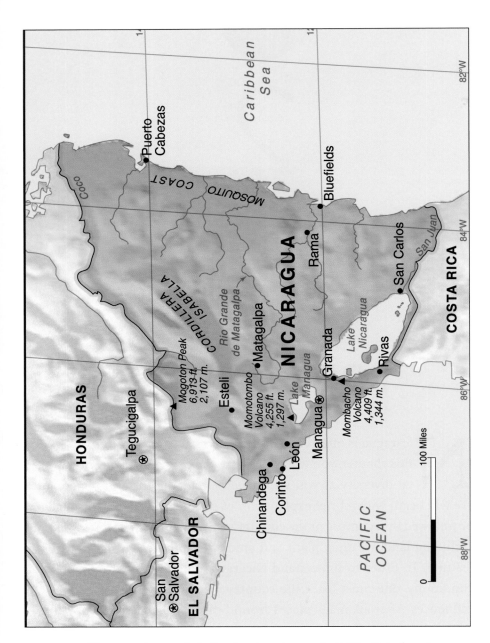

Nicaragua has varied climates, terrains, and wildlife. Rain forest covers more than 7,722 square miles (20,000 sq km), and nearly one-fifth of the country has been allocated as protected areas, or national parks and nature and biological reserves.

segments of Earth's outer crust are "floating" about and crashing into one another. Two such plates have been responsible for the formation of Central America. The Cocos Plate, located off Nicaragua's west coast, is sliding eastward at a rate of about 2.75 inches (7 centimeters) each year. This may not seem like much, but in terms of plate movement, it is extremely fast. Meanwhile, the Caribbean Plate is moving westward at about one-third of an inch (0.8 cm) annually. Like two giant bulldozers pushing toward one another, they have created at least part of the mountainous backbone of Nicaragua and the rest of Central America. Landscapes formed by the collision of plates are folded, resulting in an accordionlike series of roughly parallel mountains and valleys (much like Appalachia in the eastern United States).

Central America also lies within an extremely unstable zone prone to earthquakes and volcanic eruptions. The area is part of a much larger system called the Pacific Ring of Fire. This horseshoe-shaped belt is formed by the movement of many tectonic plates. All together, they create the most hazardous region in the world. About 75 percent of the world's volcanoes are within the Ring of Fire, many of which remain active today. And, about 90 percent of the world's earthquakes occur in this ring around the Pacific. Nicaragua lies squarely in this zone, and as a result, it is home to a number of volcanoes. In fact, there are about 20 of them, a half dozen of which remain active today. The country also experiences frequent and often devastating earthquakes (discussed in detail later in this chapter).

WEATHER AND CLIMATE

Because of its position close to the equator, Nicaragua experiences tropical conditions. Temperatures are fairly constant throughout the year, but rainfall varies greatly from season to season. As a result, the country's climate is classified as being wet-and-dry tropical.

Temperatures

By definition, tropics are those areas in which the average temperature of the coldest month is above 64.4°F (18°C). Here, temperatures change very little from season to season, remaining hot and muggy throughout the year. The temperature difference between night and day far exceeds the difference from season to season. "Nighttime," it is often said, "is the winter of the tropics." In the tropics, conditions are very monotonous. Imagine a hot, humid July day with the temperature around 90°F (32°C) and the relative humidity above 90 percent. How would you like to spend your entire lifetime with almost every day pretty much like that?

In most tropical lands, including Nicaragua, major differences in temperature are the result of elevation. Elevation is the primary control of temperature and differences in moisture within Nicaragua. Generally speaking, temperatures tend to drop about 3.5°F with each 1,000-foot increase in altitude (0.65°C per 100 meters). This is why snow remains throughout the year on many high peaks around the world (although not in Nicaragua). More than two centuries ago, German geographer Alexander von Humboldt recognized the importance of differences in temperature according to altitude. He developed a way to classify temperature zones according to altitude, called vertical zonation, that is still widely used today.

In Humboldt's classification, the *tierra caliente* ("hot land") extends from sea level to about 2,500 feet (762 meters). Here, seasonal daytime temperatures range from about 92°F (33°C) during the warm season to around 86°F (30°C) during the cooler part of the year. At night, temperatures drop to a pleasant 70°F to 75°F (21°C to 24°C). April and May, the end of the dry season, are the warmest months of the year.

At elevations ranging between about 2,500 and 5,250 feet (762 to 1,600 m) conditions are quite comfortable. This is the *tierra templada* ("temperate land"). Daytime high temperatures are a pleasant 75°F to 80°F (24°C to 27°C), and nights are a cool

Vertical Zonation at the Equator

18,000 ft. (5,500 m)	Always below freezing Permanent snow and glacial ice
15,000 ft. (4,500 m)	**Very cold sub-polar conditions Few people and vegetation**
10,000 ft. (3,000 m)	**Cool to cold Grasses and scrub – Grazing**
6,000 ft. (1,800 m)	**Cooler mid-latitude conditions Settlement, forests, hardy crops**
3,500 ft. (1,000 m)	**Quite pleasant "eternal spring" Settlement, forests, agriculture**
Sea level	**Hot and wet Rain forest, tropical subsistence farming and plantations**

© Infobase Publishing

This vertical zonation diagram illustrates the changes in climate from sea level to the top of a mountain in the equatorial region. At higher peaks in wet-tropical regions, temperatures drop about 3.5°F with every 1,000-foot increase in elevation (10°C per 1,000 meters), and peaks remain snow or ice capped throughout the year. Because of its latitudinal position, Nicaragua's temperatures differ somewhat with attitude from those at the equator.

but still enjoyable 60°F to 70°F (15°C to 21°C). At high elevations, above 5,250 feet (1,600 m), temperatures are much cooler. Daytime highs seldom rise above 75°F (24°C), and at night the temperature can plunge to a shivering (for the tropics!) 60°F (15°C) or lower. And, yes, it has been cold enough for snow to fall at higher elevations in Nicaragua—as it did in 1972!

Rainfall

Unlike temperatures, rainfall amounts vary greatly in Nicaragua, both seasonally and from region to region. Seasonal patterns in moisture are the result of seasonally shifting belts of air pressure. During the summer (high sun) part of the year, conditions that contribute to year-round heavy rainfall in the wet tropics shift northward to cover Central America. This is the wet season during which rain falls daily in some locations. In the winter (low sun) months, conditions are much drier. A high-pressure belt that creates much drier conditions in Mexico and the southwestern United States throughout the year shifts southward during this season. From December through March, very little rain falls in the Western Lowlands. (Because of the constantly blowing northeast trade winds, the Caribbean lowlands receive rain year-round, with a slight peak in summer.)

Precipitation amounts also diminish from east to west. The Eastern Lowlands fall under the influence of the northeast trade winds throughout the year. These reliable winds bring evaporated moisture from the warm tropical waters of the Caribbean. Most of the rain here, as elsewhere, falls in the form of thundershowers. Such storms can be violent, with torrential rainfall amounting to several inches, but they also tend to be quite brief in duration. This soggy region receives up to 250 inches (635 cm) of rainfall each year. By the time the winds have crossed the Eastern Lowland region and central mountain ranges, they have lost much of their moisture. Therefore, the most heavily populated western portion of the country receives much less rainfall, about 40 to 60 inches (100 to 150 cm) annually.

PLANT AND ANIMAL LIFE

Flora and fauna vary, depending on rainfall and human disturbance. Rain forests with a rich and diverse array of trees, other plants, and animal life dominate the Eastern Lowlands. In the Central Highlands, flora and fauna vary with elevation. Drier conditions and high population density account for still different biota (the combined flora and fauna of a region) in the western part of the country. During recent decades, Nicaraguans have begun to recognize and appreciate the unique nature of their natural environment. Today, the country has more than

18 percent of its territory sheltered by more than 70 wildlife reserves designed to protect its remarkable biodiversity.

Flora

Dense tropical rain forest covers much of the eastern (Atlantic) half of Nicaragua. Here, the tallest trees, called emergents, may tower 200 feet (60 m) above the forest floor. More than 100 tree species may occupy a small area. Thousands of other plants cling to their tree host much like decorations on a Christmas tree. Strangely, the forest floor itself is relatively free of plant life. The dense canopy formed by tree crowns limits sunlight and photosynthesis, and therefore, plant growth. The tree canopy instead creates an eerie green lighting on the forest floor.

It is incorrect to refer to rain forest as "jungle." Jungle is defined as a very dense, perhaps even impenetrable, growth of vegetation. The rain forest, as noted above, is relatively free of ground-level flora. Jungle is found, however, where sunlight can strike the ground, such as along streams or in clearings such as a village, field, or road.

Farther inland from the coast, oaks, pines, and other species cover the Nicaraguan highlands. In the uplands there is an elevation where fog is almost constant. This region is called the cloud forest, a fairylandlike landscape of trees, mosses, ferns, orchids, and an abundance of other flora.

In the drier and heavily populated west, plant life is sparser and highly changed by human activity. Scrubland and savanna—a mixture of tall grasses and scattered trees—exist where the land has not been disturbed by farming, settlement, or some other clearing.

Along both coasts, mangroves thrive in brackish water. The stilt-rooted plant protects coasts from erosion and also provides a sheltering ecosystem in which many organisms thrive. During recent years, severe storms have taken their toll on mangroves, particularly on the Atlantic side of Nicaragua. Fortunately, if protected, the mangrove stands will regenerate.

Fauna

Nicaragua is blessed with an abundance of animal life. There are nearly 700 species of birds, including the spectacular national bird, the *guardabarranco*, or Turquoise-Browed Motmot. Other birds include parrots, toucans, and macaws, all of which are very colorful—and loud! Big cat species include the jaguar and cougar. Smaller felines include the tree- and ground-dwelling jaguarondi, the tree-dwelling margay, and the primarily ground-bound ocelot. A variety of other animals include hard-shelled, insect-eating armadillos; strange, slow-moving three-toed sloths; the tamandua (or collared) anteater, an animal 4 feet (1.2 m) long that uses its huge claws to dig away at ant hills; and wild boars with their dangerous tusks. There are also several species of monkeys, most notably the gangly spider monkey and incredibly loud howler monkey.

The largest of Nicaragua's wild animals are the strange-looking tapir and even stranger manatee. Tapirs are land animals that seem to have had difficulty deciding what they want to be. In various aspects the tapir resembles a pig, a horse, and an elephant! The animal is about 3 feet (1 m) in height and up to 7 feet (2 m) in length, weighing up to 700 pounds (300 kilograms). Manatees live entirely in the water and are the largest of the Nicaraguan fauna. These huge animals can reach 15 feet (4.6 m) in length and weigh up to 3,300 pounds (1,500 kg). Both the tapir and manatee are increasingly rare and endangered.

Nicaragua is also home to more than 200 species of reptiles. They include more than 100 varieties of snakes, about 20 of which can be deadly. There are huge boa constrictors, a number of deadly vipers including the bushmaster (the largest venomous snake in the Americas, with a length up to 14 feet [4.7 m]), and coral snakes. Most deadly of all is the Pacific sea snake, which, fortunately, is nonagressive. Among the many other reptiles are iguanas and poison dart frogs. The latter earned their name because of their toxic secretion, which was

The tapir inhabits the forests of South and Central America and Southeast Asia. Most tapirs are about 7 feet (2 meters) long and about 3 feet high, weighing up to 700 pounds. They can live up to 30 years in the wild and in zoos.

used by Amerindians to poison the tips of blowgun darts. There are also some 2,500 species of insects in the country—a considerable number of which bite. This includes malaria-transmitting mosquitoes.

The country also has abundant aquatic life, in both fresh and salt water. The Nicaraguan shark that occupies the San Juan River and Lake Nicaragua is the world's only freshwater shark. Marine life includes an abundance of fish, shellfish, crustaceans, and green turtles.

WATER FEATURES

In addition to facing both the Atlantic and Pacific oceans, Nicaragua has many lakes and rivers. The two largest lakes occupy a large geologic trench. Lake Nicaragua (also called Cocibolca) is the largest freshwater body in Central America and the second largest in all of Latin America. (Only Lake Titicaca, in South America's Central Andes, is larger.) It is about 175 miles (282 km) long and 75 miles (121 km) wide at its widest point. The lake occupies an area of about 3,100 square miles (8,000 sq km), about the same size as Utah's Great Salt Lake during normal conditions. Because of a large and growing population and lack of adequate sewage disposal facilities, Lake Nicaragua has become increasingly polluted during recent decades.

Lake Nicaragua drains into the Caribbean Sea by way of the San Juan River. Although the lake drains eastward into the Atlantic Basin, the Pacific Ocean is nearby as well. It can be seen from atop mountains on Ometepe, the largest and highest of the lake's some 400 islands. As early as 1826, there were discussions of building a canal that would link the two oceans by using the navigable San Juan River, Lake Nicaragua, and a short canal. The canal would be cut across the Rivas Isthmus, which has a low elevation of 184 feet (56 m) and is roughly 30 miles (18 km) wide. Although the construction of the Panama Canal weakened interest in a water route across Nicaragua, the idea continues to be brought up on occasion.

Lake Managua is the country's second-largest freshwater body. It is linked to Lake Nicaragua by the Tipitapa River. It is about 40 miles (65 km) long and 15 miles (25 km) wide. Nicaragua's capital and largest city, Managua, faces upon and nearly encircles the lake. The lake's name comes from the joining of *Mangue* (the Spanish name for an Amerindian tribe) and *agua* (water). Today, the lake is extremely polluted by urban sewage and industrial toxins.

There are 10 large rivers that flow eastward into the Caribbean across the sparsely populated Eastern Lowlands. The largest is Rio Coco (or Segovia), which forms much of the border between Honduras and Nicaragua. The largest river in all of Central America, it is navigable for 140 miles (225 km) upstream from its mouth. Rio Grande de Matagalpa is the second-largest stream. Neither river has a seaport at or near its mouth. Although a number of streams have conditions suitable for building hydroelectric dams, hydroelectric development in the country has lagged. Nonetheless, in the future, energy-starved Nicaragua has the potential to develop this clean and inexpensive alternative to costly imported energy.

NATURAL DISASTERS

Nicaragua has suffered from nature's fury many times. It also has many environmental issues that result from human activity. Few countries in the Western Hemisphere are more prone to destruction wrought by environmental events or human-caused degradation.

Hurricanes

Between 1971 and 2009, 11 hurricanes or tropical storms struck the Nicaraguan coast. One, Tropical Storm Alma in 2008, struck the Pacific coast, the first to do so since 1968. The other 10 storms swept in from the Caribbean. These often devastating examples of nature's wrath occur from June through October. Winds often exceed 100 miles per hour (160 km per hour). Flimsy buildings, trees and other vegetation (including most agricultural crops), as well as wires and other infrastructure can easily be destroyed by the ferocious winds. Wind-pushed water, called a storm surge, can crash ashore with heights of up to 20 feet (6 m). The surge, in addition to extremely high waves, can destroy everything along the coast. This is one reason why the Caribbean coast of Nicaragua is so sparsely settled. Often, the greatest hurricane damage is inflicted by torrential rains that result in severe floods.

Of the many hurricanes to strike Nicaragua, none was more devastating than Hurricane Mitch in 1998. Mitch roared across the Atlantic Basin with sustained winds of 180 mph (285 kph). By the time it reached the Central American coast, the storm's winds had subsided, but the storm's movement also had slowed. Between October 28 and November 3, Mitch—by this point downgraded to a tropical storm—hovered over Nicaragua. Rain fell constantly, with some places receiving as much as 75 inches (190 cm)—more than 6 feet (2 m)—during the six-day period!

The combined destruction caused by wind, flooding, and mud slides amounted to more than $1 billion. An estimated 3,800 Nicaraguans lost their lives, many more were injured, and as many as 800,000 people were left homeless. Nearly a third of the coffee crop was destroyed, and banana, sugar, and bean crops were severely damaged. The greatest destruction occurred in the far northwestern corner of Nicaragua. There, a crater lake atop Casita, a dormant volcano, filled to overflowing. As a result, part of the volcano wall collapsed, sending a river of mud careening down the mountain slope and into valleys below. The flow buried an area roughly 10 miles long and 5 miles wide (16 km long by 8 km wide) in mud. More than 2,000 of the country's storm-related fatalities were in farms and villages near the volcano.

Earthquakes

Because it lies astride the volatile Pacific Ring of Fire, Nicaragua experiences numerous earthquakes. During the twentieth century, three of them proved to be extremely destructive and deadly. In 1931, 2,000 people lost their lives in Managua when an earthquake with a magnitude of 6.0 on the Richter scale struck the city. (The Richter scale measures the energy released by an earthquake.)

In 1972, the earth rumbled beneath Managua again. Although its intensity of 6.2 was similar to the 1931 quake, Managua's population and area had expanded greatly. By the time the quake and resulting fires had subsided, some 10,000 people were dead, more than 20,000 others were injured, and two-thirds of Managua's population, about 300,000 people, was left homeless. Most of Managua's business district and its factories were severely damaged or lay in ruin. Most of the city's emergency services, including all of the fire-fighting equipment and the city's four main hospitals, were destroyed. The city's water, power, and communication lines, as well as its roads, were in shambles. Weeks passed before even basic services were restored.

In 1992, Nicaragua experienced more devastation caused by earthquakes. That year an earthquake occurred off the Nicaraguan west coast on September 2. The quake, which was located in an active zone of stress and deformation in the earth's crust, created large tsunamis (tidal waves) and was the first tsunami earthquake to be recorded on modern broadband seismic networks. Tsunami waves that hit the area reached heights of 9.8 to 32 feet (3 to 10 m).

The people most affected by this devastating event were those living in extremely poor communities beside the sea. The people there lived on grains grown from their own farms, which were wiped out by the tsunami. Fisherpeople in the village lost their fishing equipment, boats, and storage sheds. The United Nations Disaster Relief Organization (UNDRO) mission surveyed the area and estimated that 40,500 people living in 27 communities were directly and indirectly impacted by the tsunami. At least 170 people were killed, mostly children who were asleep at the time. More than 68 people went missing, 489 were injured, and 13,500 were left homeless. The total cost of damages was estimated at between $20 million and $30 million.

Do we ever learn from experience? Many of the world's cities sprawl over hazard zones that have proven to be deadly. San Francisco, California; Galveston, Texas; and New Orleans, Louisiana, are examples. After being all but destroyed by various natural disasters, these cities rebuilt on the same sites. Managua, which is built upon a very active geologic fault, has rebuilt not once, but twice. Residents can only wonder when— not *if*—the earth beneath their feet will begin to shake, rattle, and roll once again.

On September 2, 1992, a major earthquake followed by several strong aftershocks caused a series of tidal waves of up to 32 feet (10 m) along a 136-mile (220-km) section of the Pacific coast of Nicaragua. There was not enough time to warn the coastal residents because the tsunami source was too close and it only took 20 minutes for the first destructive waves to reach the coast. Pictured, residents of Casares walk past the rubble of the Hotel Casares the day after the disaster.

ENVIRONMENTAL ISSUES

As is true of many countries, Nicaragua suffers from a number of environmental problems. Deforestation, or the cutting down or clearing away of trees and forests, is widespread in many upland areas. This, in turn, contributes to rapid run-off of rainfall and results in severe flooding in places. Many wildlife species are declining in number, some to the point of near extinction. Soil erosion is widespread, and many streams and lakes are polluted, some severely.

Furthermore, Nicaragua's cities face sanitation problems. A clean city is costly, a luxury that only wealthier societies can afford. Managua, with a population of more than one million, does not have sewage treatment. Garbage disposal is hit or miss, with many communities lacking facilities altogether.

Clearly, Nicaragua faces many serious problems relating to its natural environment. And as you have read, not all hazards are caused by nature. Humans are doing many things that degrade the environment or make it unsafe.

3

Nicaragua Through Time

Historians generally focus their studies on events, people, and dates. To the geographer, history is somewhat different. We go far back into the deep recesses of time and look for any and all evidence that sheds light on human activity, whether ancient or present day. In this chapter, you will learn more about those events that, through time, have helped to shape Nicaragua's present-day geographic conditions.

EARLIEST HUMANS

It is not known when the earliest humans set foot on the land that is today's Nicaragua. It is assumed that the Americas were initially populated by people who came from Asia and then spread out across the North and South American continents. Following this idea, Nicaragua may have been settled a very long time ago. There is evidence (although controversial) that humans may have reached eastern Brazil and southern Chile more than 30,000 years ago. It is assumed that their route would have taken them either through Central America or along its coast.

Unfortunately, the earliest humans in Nicaragua left no trace of their presence. Tropical conditions rapidly destroy or conceal most artifacts and other evidence of an early human presence. Some scientists believe that the first Americans may have followed the coast. Here, too, there are problems. The sea was several hundred feet lower 30,000 years ago than it is today. This condition existed because so much ocean water was locked up on land in the form of glacial ice during the Ice Age. Therefore, if these first Americans traveled along the coast, any trace of their presence would be deep below today's ocean surface. Because of these conditions, it is all but impossible to tell who were the earliest visitors, where they came from, when they were there, or where they went. There is no evidence to suggest that they remained in Nicaragua or elsewhere in Central America.

MYSTERIOUS FOOTPRINTS

In 1874, a construction worker accidentally made a discovery that would rock the archaeological world to its foundation. Ancient human footprints were found deeply buried beneath beds of rock near the city of Managua and the shore of Lake Managua. They appeared to have been left by people who were running for their lives—toward the lake. Scientists believed that they were running toward Lake Managua to escape the searing heat of a volcanic eruption, but now think they were collecting food and water. This eruption and many more over the millennia buried the footprints beneath up to 11 layers of volcanic ash. What came to be known as "the Ancient Footprints of Acahualinca" were found 16 to 24 feet (4.9 to 7.3 m) below the surface. Who left them? How long ago did someone walk (or run) barefoot through the mud? The controversy was just beginning!

Six-thousand-year-old footprints (*above*), called the Ancient Footprints of Acahualinca, were left behind by a group of about 10 Paleo-Indians while on their way to collect food and water. Volcanic ash that had rained down on the footprints perfectly preserved them, making them the oldest human footprints to be found on the American continent.

Originally, the footprints were dated at a staggering 200,000 years ago. The ancient date was a huge blow to both the scientific community and Christians. At the time, most archaeologists believed that humans had been in the Americas for no more than perhaps 5,000 to 6,000 years. Christian creationists believe in the literal interpretation of the Bible, that humankind in general had been around for no more than about 6,000 years.

Science came to the rescue. The feet were found to be those of "modern" humans, no more than about 50,000 years old. Soon, new technology made it possible to date the prints to 10,000 years or younger. Finally, radiocarbon dating gave a fairly precise age of 5,945 years plus or minus 145 years.

So, it appears that the footprints were left sometime around 4000 B.C. Today, casts of these footprints are on display at the National Museum in Washington, D.C., and also at the Peabody Museum of Archaeology at Harvard University in Cambridge, Massachusetts. The Museum of Acahualinca, located in the west of Managa, displays the actual footprints along with a small collection of pottery and other ancient objects including mammoth footprints, traditional tools made before European influence, and a skull from the historic town of Léon Viejo.

PALEO-INDIANS

In terms of the archaeological record, including the ancient footprints, the earliest documented date of settlement in Nicaragua was about 4000 B.C., or about 6,000 years ago. It is important to note that in the tropics, nearly all artifacts decompose rapidly in the tropical heat and humidity. Those that are more durable are difficult, if not impossible, to find because of the very dense vegetation. When the Spaniards arrived in the early 1500s, nearly all material possessions, including houses and weapons (swords, lances, and arrows, as well) were made of wood. Therefore, archaeologists have very few remains of any kind that provide clues that can shed light on a more ancient human presence.

It is believed that most early cultures hunted, fished, and gathered for their livelihood. They lived in a land that offered rich opportunities for these subsistence activities. Because of the abundant resources, it is doubtful that they were nomads, roaming from place to place in search of food and water. Rather, they probably lived in one place, forming small communities occupied by extended families, or perhaps several families. Through time, some Amerindians began to farm. They practiced a form of early slash-and-burn cultivation, which is still commonplace within tropical environments today. Slash-and-burn cultivation is the cutting and burning of forests or woodlands to create fields for agriculture or land for livestock. Increased food production made it possible for both population and settlements to grow in size.

INDIGENOUS PEOPLES AT THE TIME OF CONQUEST

When the Spaniards arrived in the early sixteenth century, Nicaragua was home to several indigenous groups with quite different backgrounds. They included the Niquirano, Chorotegano, and Chontal. Tribal groups in the western and central portions of what is today Nicaragua had close cultural ties to the Aztecs and the Mayans of modern-day Mexico. Those of the Eastern Lowlands had closer cultural links with the Chibcha, whose homeland was to the south in present-day Panama and Colombia. Their levels of cultural development also varied greatly. Let's take a brief look at the various groups as they were at the time of European contact.

People of the Western Lowlands and Central Highlands

Generally speaking, indigenous cultures of the Western Lowlands were quite well developed. Most of the languages were dialects of Pipil, a tongue closely related to Nahuatl, the language of the Aztecs in Mexico. The culture of the Western Lowlands included productive agriculture, cities, and an advanced form of political organization grouped around small kingdoms. All three of these traits suggest a cultural link between the western Nicaraguan Amerindians and the Aztecs. So, too, do the staple foods of the Nicaraguans. Maize (corn), beans, squash, avocados, and fiery hot chili peppers were the most common foods then (and now). Meat came from hunting and fishing, in addition to domestic turkeys and—are you ready for this?—dogs that were raised as food. All of these foods formed the foundation of the Aztec diet.

Some groups of the Central Highlands appeared to have closer cultural ties to the Mayan people of southern Mexico and eastern Guatemala. The Chontal were the primary group

living in the central uplands. They were less advanced culturally than were the groups occupying the Western Lowlands.
Most eked out a meager living by hunting and gathering or
practicing low-yielding slash-and-burn shifting farming.

People of the Eastern Caribbean Lowlands

People of the Eastern Lowlands migrated northward from
Colombia sometime in the distant past. They speak languages
related to Chibchan, which is the language of indigenous peoples in northern Colombia and Panama. In the early sixteenth
century, most of the Amerindians of the Caribbean lowlands
still subsisted on foods from hunting, fishing, and gathering. Rather than village life, they lived in small groups that
were widely scattered about the eastern lowland region. Some
practiced slash-and-burn agriculture, which made village life
possible. For the farmers, important foods included plantains
(a bananalike plant and fruit that is cooked), cassava (a root
crop), and pineapples.

IS THE NAME "AMERICA" NICARAGUAN IN ORIGIN?

The name "America" first appeared in 1507 on a map credited
to Martin Waldseemüller, a mapmaker who lived in northeastern France. Most historians believe that Waldseemüller
adopted the name from Albericus (or Alberico, or Morinto)
Vespucius (also spelled Vespuchy, Vespucci, or Vespuzio). As
early as 1885, an intriguing countertheory was suggested by
Jules Marcou, a Swiss geologist. He believed that Waldseemüller could only have known Vespucci by the names Albericus
or Alberico. Neither of these, of course, sounds like "America."
The place-naming practices of the time cast further doubt on
the traditional theory of America's name origin. The custom
was to use only the *last* names of explorers or other individuals
as place names. There are many variations of Columbus, for
example (e.g., Columbia, Colombia, Colón, Colombo), but no
place name that incorporates the explorer's first name.

If not from Vespucci, where might the name "America" have come from? There is an interesting alternative theory, also first suggested by Jules Marcou and supported by the research of others. Amerique (with various spellings) is the name given by Amerindians to the range of mountains in Nicaragua that bears the same name today. During his fourth voyage, which began in 1502, Columbus noted that the wooden hulls of his ships were "badly worm-eaten and . . . leaking alarmingly." The damage had been caused by teredo worms. In order to repair the damage to his vessels, Columbus and his crew put ashore for 11 days. Most historians place his landfall in Costa Rica, but meticulous research by Nicaraguan archaeologist Jorge Espinosa Estrada has shown conclusively that it was along the coast of Nicaragua.

Columbus's major objective, of course, was to find wealth, particularly gold. The Amerindians with whom Columbus came in contact were richly adorned with ornaments made from the precious metal. Certainly, the Spaniards would have asked where the gold came from. What would have been the Amerindians' response? "Amerique!" The Sierra Amerique was a major source of the precious metal, not only to the Native population, but to later Spanish colonists.

When Columbus returned, it is very possible that "Amerique" had become a synonym for the distant and newly discovered land across the Atlantic in which gold was abundant. Gradually, news of the vast mineral wealth and the name of the location at which it was found would have begun to spread from seaport to seaport. Within several years, the name probably reached St. Dié, a community in northeastern France. There, excited by the new information, Waldseemüller incorporated it on his now famous map. If this hypothesis is true, worms played a significant role in the naming of America. And, of even greater importance, the name itself is Nicaraguan in origin.

EARLY SPANISH ERA

Although Columbus may have put ashore in Nicaragua in 1502, the first well-documented Spanish visitor was Gil González

Dávila. Traveling northward from Panama, González and his troops reached the land that ultimately became Nicaragua in 1522. They explored the western part of the region. While there, they discovered two large lakes and found the Native peoples to be quite civilized. Initially, the Amerindians there treated González and his troops warmly. Many of them were even baptized into the Roman Catholic faith by the small party of Spanish explorers.

The Spaniard's primary mission in the Americas was to discover gold and other mineral wealth. You can imagine their surprise and pleasure when Chief Nicarao gave gold—and lots of it—to the party leader. González was greatly impressed with the reception given to him and his troops by the Native peoples. Not only had they given him gold, but he also had been successful in converting them to Christianity.

Swelled with success and confidence, González and his troops moved into the region's interior. This, however, proved to be a huge and almost fatal mistake. There, his small group was savagely attacked by some 3,000 hostile Amerindians. He and his men fled for their lives, retreating to the coast where they had anchored their three ships, now leaky. (Those teredo worms again!) In June 1523, the group returned to Panama. González told of the highly developed cultures and large cities he had discovered; and, of course, he had a large amount of gold and pearls brought from the land newly named "Nicaragua." As you can imagine, his return created "gold fever" among many Spanish *conquistadors* (conquerors).

Within a matter of months, several different groups of gold-hungry Spanish forces invaded Nicaragua. González returned, with support of the Spanish Crown. Francisco Hernández de Córdoba was sent by the governor of Panama. There were others, including Cristóbal de Olid, who was sent south by Hernán Cortés, the conqueror of Mexico. De Olid came from the north, entering Nicaragua from Honduras. Whereas most invaders were interested only in gold, Córdoba came with more permanent goals: He wanted to colonize

Sent in 1524 to claim Nicaragua for Spain, explorer and slave trader Francisco Hernández de Córdoba founded the first permanent Spanish settlements in Central America–Granada and León. Córdoba was killed by Pedro Arias Dávila, the governor of Panama, when he tried to claim Nicaragua for himself. Today, the currency of Nicaragua is called the córdoba.

Nicaragua. In order to accomplish this, he needed to establish towns. In 1524, he founded Granada on the western shore of Lake Nicaragua.

The city of Granada holds the distinction of being the oldest continuously settled Spanish settlement on the mainland of the Americas. Soon after its establishment, several other communities were settled, including León, located northwest of Lake Managua, just inland from the Pacific coast.

As so often was the case during the Spanish conquest of Latin America, would-be conquistadors violently fought against one another. This was the case in Nicaragua. The seemingly inevitable clash—called the War of the Captains—

not only pitted Spanish forces against each other, but also involved Amerindians. By the time it was over, the indigenous population was wiped out and their cities and civilization lay in ruin.

By 1527, Nicaragua was under Spain's firm grip. Many of the fortune- and power-seeking conquistadors, including Córdoba, were dead. They had been killed in battle or murdered or executed for various offenses. (Execution, often for some trumped-up offense, was a common way for a ruler to rid himself of competition.) After the dust settled and the conquest was complete, Pedro Arias Dávila became the colony's first governor. He located his capital at León and ruled until his death of natural causes at the age of 91 in 1531.

CONSEQUENCES ON NATIVE PEOPLES

It is estimated that at the time of early Spanish contact, as many as one million Amerindians lived in what is now Nicaragua. Within three decades, only an estimated 100,000 remained in the country—a horrendous loss of about 90 percent of the indigenous population. Many factors contributed to the massive decline in population. First, many Amerindians were killed in skirmishes with the Spaniards. They were no match for the invaders' horses, armor, guns, and other weapons.

Second, Amerindians had no immunity to Old World diseases. Smallpox, mumps, measles, chicken pox, influenza, and even the common cold took a terrible toll on people who had not previously been exposed to them. Contact was particularly devastating to Amerindians in western and central Nicaragua, where most Spaniards lived. Because of its steaming climate, rain-forest vegetation, and the lack of gold, Spaniards tended to avoid the Eastern Lowland region. Therefore, many people living in that area survived. Third, between the late 1520s and 1540, an estimated 200,000 Amerindians were enslaved and sent to South America to work in mines in Peru and elsewhere.

Another major consequence of early contact was biological. The Spaniards were soldiers of fortune who came alone. Most planned to get rich (by finding gold) and return home, but very few actually did. Eventually, they took wives from among the Amerindian population. Their children of mixed European and Native American ancestry are called mestizos in Spanish. Today, nearly 7 of every 10 Nicaraguans claim this mixed background. Finally, religious conversion was but the beginning of a massive cultural exchange that in time markedly altered both indigenous and Spanish ways of life.

EARLY COLONIAL ERA

After the conquest, many Spaniards settled in the western part of the country. They were attracted by the region's gold, fertile valleys, large lakes, and volcanic mountains. The climate was somewhat drier (and therefore more pleasant) than the muggy tropical lowlands of the east, and the land was not covered by dense rain forest. There also were many more Amerindians. Spaniards who had participated in the conquest often received parcels of land in return for their service, but they had little taste for manual labor. Rather, Amerindians were enslaved to work the fields, tend the livestock, and perform other tasks involving hard manual labor.

From almost the beginning of the colonial era, Spain actually showed little interest in Nicaragua. It was far more interested in plundering the vast riches found in Mexico and Peru. In fact, by the early 1530s, many of the initial Spanish settlers had left Nicaragua, and a number of the small Spanish-settled communities had vanished. By the end of the sixteenth century, only León and Granada remained as Spanish urban centers.

In 1544, Nicaragua became part of the new Captaincy General of Guatemala, which was a region within the Viceroyalty of New Spain. This division included all Spanish holdings in Central America. As the name implies, the various provinces were governed from Guatemala. Each province had its own *alcalde mayor* (governor). León was selected as Nicaragua's provincial capital. It was the center not only of government, but of other important functions and appointees as well. These included various economic activities and the Catholic archdiocese and bishop.

COLONIAL ERA TO INDEPENDENCE

During the 1600s, economic and political life in the province was in the firm grasp of a Creole elite. (Creoles were people born in the New World of Spanish descent.) Times were hard. Spain had little interest in this part of its empire, so it largely neglected its Central American holdings. Gold production was dwindling as ores petered out. Agricultural production was experiencing a sharp decline. Early in the colonial era, most Spaniards had little interest in farming or livestock ranching. After all, both involved hard labor, something alien to the Spaniards' experience. The Amerindian population had all but died out, so there were few people to be enslaved.

Most rulers of the province were interested only in increasing their own wealth and power. They had little interest in improving the well-being of the people over whom they governed. In Nicaragua, like in most other Latin American countries, a huge gap existed between the wealthy elite and the impoverished masses.

Nature, too, was harsh. In 1610, the violent eruption of the volcano Momotombo destroyed León, the capital. The city was rebuilt at a new site to the northwest and at a greater distance from the restless volcano. During the mid-1600s, three devastating earthquakes also caused massive and widespread destruction within Nicaragua.

By and large, Nicaragua remained little changed during the colonial era. There were, however, several conditions or events that played a major role in the country's historical development. One was the constant and often-violent rivalry between the conservative elite of Granada and the liberal elite of León.

This conflict lasted for centuries and in some respects continues to the present day. (Nicaragua's politics are discussed in detail in Chapter 5.)

During the latter half of the seventeenth century, Nicaragua began to be harassed by outsiders. French, British, and Dutch pirates frequently raided Nicaragua's coastal regions. On two occasions pirate raiders even ventured inland, where they attacked the city of Granada. The British had long had their eyes on the Caribbean coastal zone and in 1687, they laid claim to Nicaragua's Miskito Coast. Spain hotly contested the British claim, as did Nicaragua after its independence. Nonetheless, the Miskito Coast was under foreign control (or briefly autonomous) until 1894, when Nicaragua regained control of the region.

By the eighteenth century, the Spanish had mined most of the mineral riches in Central America. They began to turn their attention to agriculture—raising tropical crops and livestock (primarily for leather and tallow, used in the making of candles) for export. As the colonial era began to wind down, Nicaragua was at war with itself. Any potential for progress within the country was lost due to the constant fighting between the powerful and elite conservatives of Granada and the liberals of León.

NICARAGUA BECOMES INDEPENDENT

By the early nineteenth century, most Latin American colonies were clamoring for independence. Spain had taken vast wealth from its colonies, but had given very little in return. At home, the Spanish had their own problems. The French had invaded Spain in the last decade of the eighteenth century, and the country was suffering from internal political conflict. With its attention turned elsewhere, Spain severely neglected its colonies in Central America and elsewhere in the Americas.

Nicaragua gained its independence in stages. First, the Captaincy General of Guatemala declared independence from

Spain on September 15, 1821. Although free of Spanish control, the region became part of the Mexican Empire. Few Central Americans approved of this arrangement, however, and it was short-lived. Nicaragua and four other colonies declared their independence from Mexico in 1823 and joined together to form the United Provinces of Central America. This arrangement also was destined to fail. The different units—Guatemala, El Salvador, Honduras, Nicaragua, and Costa Rica—constantly bickered among themselves. The situation became so heated that a bitter civil war broke out in 1826 and lasted until 1829. Finally, in 1837, the federation fell apart.

On its own for the first time in its history, Nicaragua acted rapidly, declaring its independence on April 30, 1838.

PERIOD OF U.S. INTEREST

When gold was discovered in California in the mid-nineteenth century, there was a massive rush to the "Golden State." From the eastern United States, the trip could be made directly by land, by water around the southern tip of South America, or by a combination of water and land travel. The latter strategy involved a Central American crossing, usually across the narrow Isthmus of Panama.

Cornelius Vanderbilt, a wealthy American who made a fortune in shipping and railroads, had another idea. He opened a route across the Nicaraguan isthmus. Boats were used on the San Juan River and Lake Nicaragua, followed by a narrow land crossing between the lake and the Pacific Ocean. Vanderbilt's route saved about 600 miles (965 km) of travel compared to the Panama route and cut the price of passage by half. Plans for an all-water canal across Nicaragua were hotly debated for a half-century, primarily by Americans and British interests, but they never materialized. Ultimately, an all-water canal across Panama opened in 1914.

Following independence, politics in Nicaragua were turbulent, a condition that in many respects continues today. One key figure during this era was José Santos Zelaya, who served as Nicaragua's president from 1893 until 1909. During his presidency, he was able to achieve some positive results. The country's economy grew. He built railroads and established steamship lines. He put in place a number of progressive programs including the improvement of public education and strengthening constitutional rights. In 1894, Zelaya regained control of the Miskito Coast.

Zelaya also meddled extensively in the affairs of Nicaragua's neighbors. He hoped to reunite Nicaragua and its neighboring countries as the United States of Central America. Zelaya, of course, envisioned himself as the new country's president. As you can imagine, this did not sit well with the other Central American countries and leaders! He also managed to antagonize the United States. The United States had thrown its support behind the building of a canal in Panama. Still hoping for a trans-Nicaraguan canal, Zelaya sought help from foreign lands, including Germany and Japan. The United States saw its economic and political interests in the region being threatened. In 1909, Zelaya was removed from office, almost certainly with some U.S. support.

With Nicaragua's political situation up in the air and the construction of the U.S.-built Panama Canal well underway, U.S. Marines entered Nicaragua in 1912. With the exception of a very brief withdrawal in 1925, they remained in the country until 1933. The U.S. presence stabilized the political situation but opened the door to what would become a political family dynasty. The Somoza family came to power in 1936 and remained in control of the country until 1979.

For Nicaragua, the twentieth century was one of almost constant turbulence. Much of the time, the country was under the control of dictators, often supported by the military. U.S. intervention in Nicaragua, whether by Marine occupational forces or other means, was frequent. During much of the last half of the twentieth century, the country was torn apart

As forty-ninth president of Nicaragua (1893–1909), José Santos Zelaya's administration had a mixed record. Although he enacted a number of progressive programs, he was also a tyrant. In 1909, Zelaya was forced out of Nicaragua, and he spent the rest of his life in exile in Mexico, Spain, and New York.

by a revolution that erupted into a lengthy and devastating civil war between conservative Sandinista and liberal Contra forces.

In order for a country and its people to prosper, there must be a stable and reliable government that is responsible to its citizens. A country's people must also work together for the common good. Neither condition has occurred in strife-torn Nicaragua. This sad tale of woe will be continued in the chapters on Nicaragua's government and economy.

4

People and Culture

N icaragua is home to nearly 6 million people. In this country, however, population density (here about 83 people per square mile, or 32 per square kilometer) is all but meaningless. Nearly 60 percent of the people live in cities, and much of the eastern half of the country supports a very sparse population.

Racially and ethnically, most Nicaraguans are of mixed Amerindian and European ancestry. About a third of the population is composed of other groups that, in small numbers, add to the country's human mosaic. This chapter focuses upon the Nicaraguan people. It begins with a look at their demographics (demography is the science that studies population statistics) and settlement (where they live). You will also learn who they are in terms of race and ethnicity. Finally, you will learn about important aspects of their culture, or way of life.

POPULATION

In mid-2009, Nicaragua's estimated population was just under 5.9 million. (This and all other demographic data appearing in this chapter are based upon U.S. government estimates. The last official Nicaraguan census was taken in 2005. For current estimates, see the *CIA World Factbook.*) Among Central American nations, this places the country in the middle in terms of numbers of people. Belize, Panama, and Costa Rica have lower populations, and El Salvador, Honduras, and Guatemala have larger populations than Nicaragua. Since Nicaragua is Central America's largest country, this may seem strange, but you must remember that a large part of the country is formed by either rugged uplands or steaming tropical lowlands. For various reasons, most Nicaraguans have avoided these difficult environments and the challenges they impose on development and settlement.

Population Change

Whether a country's population grows, remains stable, or declines is determined by four factors: births, deaths, in-migration, and out-migration. Using these criteria, changes in a country's population can be measured in a number of ways. Perhaps the most common statistic is the rate of natural (population) increase, or RNI. For Nicaragua, this figure is estimated to be about 1.8 percent per year. You must remember that this is the *natural* increase, or the percentage of population change based upon the balance of births over deaths. It does not include population change based upon migration. This means that the country's population is growing somewhat more rapidly than the world annual average gain of 1.2 percent. At this rate, Nicaragua's population (based solely upon births vs. deaths) would add about 106,200 people each year.

A country's RNI is based upon birth rates and death rates. Nicaragua experienced 23.25 births and 4.30 deaths per 1,000 people during 2009. The latter figure is the lowest in the

Americas and one of the lowest in the world. This suggests that the country's population is both young and quite healthy. A country's total fertility rate (TFR) is another way to view population change. This is the average number of children to which women give birth during their lifetime. For Nicaragua, the figure is 2.57, which is somewhat above the replacement rate of 2.1 (the .1 is explained by the fact that some women will never have children). On the other hand, Nicaragua's TFR is just a fraction below the world average. This suggests that, like most other Latin American countries, Nicaragua's population growth is slowing. This is important because it allows a country to better provide services such as health and education. A slowing population growth rate also imposes less of a burden on the country's economy.

Finally, populations can also change in response to migration. Currently, Nicaragua is experiencing a negative 1.1/1,000 migration rate. This means that about 6,500 more people leave the country than enter each year. Only a handful of countries in the Western Hemisphere are losing people to out-migration. Certainly, in the case of Nicaragua, this is a reflection of the country's poor economy and long tradition of political instability. Throughout history, people have searched for a better life as measured by economic well-being, as well as a safe and secure social and political environment. Throughout most of its history, Nicaragua has offered neither.

Demographics of Well-Being

A variety of demographic figures can provide valuable clues to the well-being of a country and its population. Perhaps the most reliable index is that of life expectancy, the average number of years a person can expect to live. For Nicaragua, the figure is 71.5 years, slightly above the world average of 66.6, but still one of the lowest in the Americas. In Nicaragua, as is true almost everywhere, women outlive men. Female life expectancy is 73.75 years, or 4.4 years longer than the 69.35 average for males.

Hundreds of thousands of Nicaraguans have left their homes for the United States, Mexico, and other Central American countries. Hoping to receive a living wage and benefit from better opportunities, migrants illegally cross the borders of Honduras and Costa Rica to work as *peons* (landless laborers) on plantations. Pictured, illegal Nicaraguan workers carry their belongings as they are led from a sugarcane field by Honduran immigration officers to be deported back to Nicaragua.

Age structure can also tell us a great deal about a country's demographics. Population pyramids (see graph on page 51) provide a viewer with a visual image of age and sex divisions of a population. As is true throughout the less-developed world, Nicaragua's population is quite young. The average Nicaraguan is a very young 22 years (versus 37 for the United States and 40 for Canada). One-third of the population is 14 or younger. On the other hand, only 3.3 percent of the people are 65 or older. For the United States and Canada, respectively, these figures

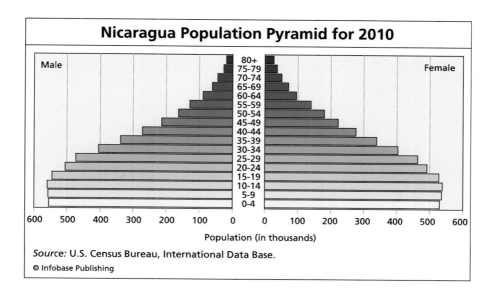

Nicaragua Population Pyramid for 2010

Male | Female

80+
75-79
70-74
65-69
60-64
55-59
50-54
45-49
40-44
35-39
30-34
25-29
20-24
15-19
10-14
5-9
0-4

600 500 400 300 200 100   0   0 100 200 300 400 500 600

Population (in thousands)

Source: U.S. Census Bureau, International Data Base.
© Infobase Publishing

are 20.2 percent and 12.8 percent age 14 and under, and 16.1 percent and 15.2 percent age 65 or older.

Certainly few statistics give a more valid indication of a country's standard of living than does its infant mortality rate, the annual number of deaths among children from birth to age one. For Nicaragua, the figure is 25 deaths per 1,000 live births, somewhat better than the world average of 46 out of 1,000. Still, it is quite high compared to the developed world, where, for example, the figures for the United States (6.6 of 1,000) and Canada (5.0 of 1,000) are much lower. Infant mortality is a very good indicator of a country's health conditions, including medical care, health services, nutrition, and sanitation.

Human Development

As you have seen, population information can tell us more than just numbers. Demographic data can reveal a great deal about the well-being of a country's people. The United Nations has developed a system for measuring human development. The Human Development Index (HDI) is a measure used to compare living standards, life expectancy, education, literacy, and other measures. Using this yardstick, Nicaragua ranks 124 among the 182 countries included in the survey. In the Western Hemisphere, only Haiti ranks lower.

Clearly, Nicaragua has a long way to go before its people enjoy a standard of living comparable to that of other countries in the Americas. One major challenge the government faces is educating its populace. Only two-thirds of Nicaraguans can read and write. Unless literacy rates are improved, the country faces an uphill battle in improving the economy and other areas of development.

SETTLEMENT

Settlement refers to where people live and how they distribute themselves across the land they occupy. As mentioned in the introduction to this chapter, population density figures for Nicaragua, as is true of most countries, are rather meaningless. The country's population density is about 83 people per square mile (32 per square kilometer). But does this figure tell us anything about *where* they live?

Only about 700,000 people, or 12 percent of the country's population, live in the vast tropical eastern part of the country. Cities are home to 58 percent of the population (this figure is well below the Latin American average of 77 percent). Nearly 1.7 million Nicaraguans, or just under 30 percent of the country's people, live in the Managua metropolitan area. As you can see, people are densely clustered in some areas and very sparsely scattered about in others.

During recent decades, the pace of internal rural-to-urban migration has increased rapidly. Since 1970, for example, Managua's population has nearly tripled. Comparable growth has been experienced by a number of the country's urban centers. The trend in Nicaragua is similar to that of many countries in the less-developed world. Most rural people are faced with inadequate or even nonexistent services, such as health care and educational opportunities. They lack transportation and communication linkages. Most of them are poor. Is it any wonder that so many of them make the decision to leave their rural home and seek a better life in the city?

NICARAGUA'S MIX OF PEOPLES

It is becoming increasingly difficult to divide people into groups. In this context, there is an extremely important distinction that must be made. *Race* refers to one's biological inheritance. For all practical purposes, it is a meaningless concept, one that many scientists (and others) have dropped. *Culture,* on the other hand, is extremely important. It is a peoples' way of life, or their learned behavior—everything they know, possess, or are able to do. People of one race can and do represent many cultures. Or (as in the United States and Canada, for example), one culture can be composed of people representing many races.

Nicaragua's population represents a mosaic of peoples. In the 2005 Nicaraguan census, when asked to identify their ancestry many people responded "Other," "Not Sure," or "Ignore." Think of your own background for a moment. How many different racial or ethnic groups are represented in your background? Today, such differences are of much less importance than in times past. Nicaraguans are mainly Amerindian, European (Caucasian), African, or mixed (mestizo) in terms of their ancestry.

Amerindians

The original people, the Amerindians, represent but a small minority today. In Chapter 3, you learned that perhaps 90 percent of the original indigenous population died or was captured and sent to South America as slaves. Today, only about 5 percent of Nicaraguans claim Amerindian ancestry. Nearly all of the indigenous population lives in the eastern lowland region where few Europeans settled. They are divided into nearly a dozen different tribal groups.

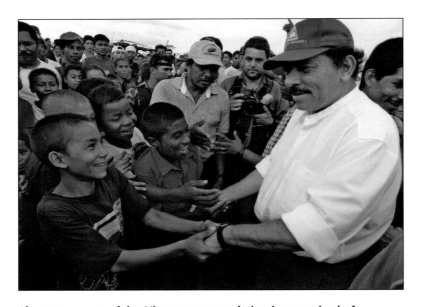

About 5 percent of the Nicaraguan population is comprised of Amerindians, or unmixed descendants of the country's original peoples. This includes the Nicarao, the Ramas, the Sumos, and the Miskito. These groups once made up a substantial indigenous minority, but their numbers have dwindled due to assimilation into the mestizo, or mixed, majority. Above, Miskito children are greeted by Nicaraguan president Daniel Ortega.

Far and away the largest group is the Miskitos, who represent about one-third of the Amerindian population. (Surprisingly, perhaps, the name has nothing to do with the pesky insect that is so common to the Miskito coastal region.) Miskito is their native tongue, although today many of them speak English or Spanish. Today, most Amerindians of the Eastern Lowlands, including the Miskitos, are of mixed ancestry. They intermarried with escaped slaves, most of whom fled to Nicaragua from various Caribbean islands.

White Europeans

Seventeen percent of the country's population claims white (European, Caucasian) ancestry. Most of them are Spanish in origin. They represent the socioeconomic "elite," a status position they have held since the conquest. There are also a small number of Germans, most of whom live in Matagalpa or other communities in the north-central mountainous area of Nicaragua. Other Europeans include small numbers of Portuguese, Italians, Belgians, and French. Most of those with European ancestry became involved in major commercial activities. Some developed sugar or coffee plantations; others went into businesses such as banking, tourism, newspapers, or brewing.

Afro-Nicaraguans

Nine percent of the Nicaraguan population claims black African ancestry. Nearly all of them live in the Eastern Lowlands bordering the Caribbean Sea. During the period when the British controlled the coastal zone, they introduced a number of laborers, mainly from their Jamaica colony. As a result, today Nicaragua has the largest number of African Americans in Central America. (Belize has a higher percentage of blacks, but the population is not as high.) A number of Eastern Lowland groups are of highly mixed ancestry.

Mestizos

Mestizos, people of mixed Amerindian and European descent, are far and away the major group in Nicaragua. Nearly 7 of every 10 Nicaraguans (or 69 percent) claim this mixed ancestry. Mestizos are found in every level of society. In Nicaragua, as elsewhere in Latin America, a person's status is based upon behavior, language (in this case, the ability to speak fluent Spanish), economic success, and education.

Others

Nicaragua also has small numbers of people from other backgrounds. For example, there are about 30,000 residents from the Middle East, including Palestinians, Jews, Syrians, and Lebanese. There are also about 12,000 Chinese Nicaraguans.

Nearly all members of these various groups live in cities and are engaged in various business activities.

LANGUAGE

In most countries that were once colonies, the language of the colonizing country remains the official tongue, even after independence. Nicaragua is no exception. (In the Western Hemisphere, the only exceptions are Ecuador, Peru, and Bolivia. In these countries, one or more of the indigenous languages is official along with Spanish.) Spanish is the official language of Nicaragua and is spoken by more than 97 percent of the people.

Small numbers of people, about 1.7 percent of the population, speak Miskito or some other indigenous tongue. Because of the long period of British control of the Caribbean coastal zone, about 50,000 Nicaraguans speak English or Creole English. Many of them speak English in addition to their native language. Creole is a form of English that incorporates words from a number of other regional tongues.

English, of course, is also spoken as a second language by many people engaged in activities that require international communication. Therefore, people involved in the tourism industry are encouraged to learn English, as are most people engaged in international commerce, media, entertainment, sports, aviation, or scientific research. Only a fraction of one percent of the country's population speaks some other language, such as Chinese or Arabic.

RELIGION

In terms of religion, and as a former Spanish colony, Nicaragua is unique. According to the 2005 national census, only 58.5 percent of the country's population is Roman Catholic, the lowest in Latin America. You may recall from Chapter 3 that Gil González Dávila, the first Spaniard to enter the interior of what became Nicaragua, converted Chief Nicaro to Catholicism. About 6,000 of Nicaro's fellow tribesmen were also converted

Although Nicaragua does not have an official religion and the government supports religious freedom and tolerance, Roman Catholicism has the largest following. Bishops are often called upon to attend state occasions and offer their opinions on various issues. There are also many schools run by Roman Catholic bodies, and yearly festivals in honor of patron saints are popular events. Above, Catholic devotees take part in the Via Crucis during Easter celebrations in Teustepe.

to the faith. Roman Catholicism was the established faith in Nicaragua until 1939. Today, however, freedom of religion is guaranteed by the Nicaraguan constitution, and the country has no official religion. During the past century, the number of people actively practicing Catholicism has declined sharply. Many people who do claim Catholicism as their faith rarely, if ever, attend worship services.

Various Protestant denominations have been more success-ful in Nicaragua than in any other Latin American country. First introduced nearly a century ago, Protestant faiths today claim about 25 percent of the country's church-going population. Evangelical groups and Moravians have been quite successful in gaining converts in the Caribbean coastal zone. Latter Day Saints (Mormons) and Jehovah's Witnesses also have been very successful in gaining converts during recent decades. About 16 percent of Nicaraguans claim no religious affiliation.

As is true in many countries, a substantial number of national holidays are based upon religious observances. Nicaragua is no exception. Christmas and Easter are major religious holidays in Nicaragua; so are several days associated with the Easter season, such as Holy Thursday and Good Friday. Others include All Souls and the Immaculate Conception holidays. To many Nicaraguans, the latter celebration is more important than Christmas. Celebrated in early December, the weeklong festivities include the building of altars to the Virgin Mary in homes and public places. Most communities also hold a gala fiesta to celebrate their patron saint.

SPORTS

Most Latin American countries claim *fútbol* (football, or what the United States calls soccer) as their most popular sport. Once again, however, Nicaragua stands apart. Here, as in the Dominican Republic, baseball, rather than football, is the most popular game. Actually, U.S.-style baseball has been popular since the late 1880s—more than 130 years ago! Today, the country supports five professional teams. It has also had its share of U.S. and Canadian major league players. The country's first Major League Baseball player was Dennis Martinez. In 1991, Martinez became the first Latin American pitcher to throw a perfect game; he was the thirteenth pitcher in history to do so. At the time, he was pitching for the Montreal Expos.

Boxing is also popular, and the country has had several world champions. Alexis Argüelo was a three-time world champion fighting in several weight classes over the years. After retiring from the ring, he became involved in politics and was elected mayor of Managua in 2008. Another boxer, Ricardo Mayorga, has also been very successful. He has held world championships in both the World Boxing Association and the World Boxing Council.

FOODWAYS

Foodways—all foods and practices associated with dining—are a fundamental aspect of any culture. Nicaraguans love to eat, and it is little wonder. They have a rich cuisine that varies from region to region. The country's cuisine has benefited from a blending of Spanish, Amerindian, and African traditions. Much of the cuisine is prepared from locally available foods. In the west, maize, meat, and local fruits are basic staples. In the east, various types of seafood, coconut and coconut milk, and tropical fruits are popular. Rice and beans are common staples in all regions of the country. Fruits, which make up an important part of the Nicaraguan diet, include mangos, papayas, bananas, and avocados. Meat includes beef, pork, and chicken. But if visiting a Nicaraguan home, particularly one in the country, don't be surprised if you are served tapir, guinea pig, turtle, or iguana.

Each region and every culture has produced its own characteristic main dish, dessert, and beverage. Through time, many of the local foods and beverages have become widely accepted throughout the country. The national dish is *gallo pinto* (or *gallopinto*), which is eaten daily by many Nicaraguans. Although it can be enjoyed as a part of any meal, it is most often a part of breakfast. As with many American dishes, there are numerous variations in its ingredients. Basically, it is made with rice, red beans, onion, and sweet peppers. Garlic and/or cilantro may be added for taste. In the Eastern Lowlands, coconut oil or grated coconut may be added. The tasty mixture is then fried. Traditional Nicaraguan recipes can be found on a number of Web sites.

NICARAGUAN CULTURE

In this chapter you have learned that Nicaraguan culture offers a rich mix of traits contributed through time by Amerindians, Europeans, Africans, and others. Each group has contributed to the country's blend of words, foods, customs, and other practices. The most dominant cultural imprint is that of the Spanish conquerors. Their language, religion, architecture, social customs, dress, and other traits are the accepted ways of living today. As you will learn in the chapters on government and economy, these essential components also suffer under Spanish-introduced and Spanish-imposed practices.

Today, Nicaraguans are beginning to awaken to a world that in many respects has passed them by. They find themselves far behind many, if not most, other Latin American countries in such vital areas as education and literacy, economic development, infrastructure, and other measures of human well-being. Much of the problem can be traced directly to Nicaragua's long history of ineffective, unresponsive, and corrupt politics. In the following chapter, you will learn how the lack of a stable government has set the country back in so many ways.

5

Government
and Politics

Acountry's government is primarily a reflection of the history and culture of the place. In the case of colonized countries, the past may be used or misused to govern the population. Thus, the tyranny of early Spanish rulers who devastated indigenous populations is not viewed as a positive example of governance.

The examination of Nicaragua's history also shows that political rule has been mainly by dictators, such as Anastasio Somoza Garcia (who ruled as the sixty-fifth and sixty-ninth president), sprinkled with a few periods of democracy. Like many other Latin American countries, Nicaragua has had its share of military leaders, dictatorships, assassinations, and outside interventions. Colonial rule and dictatorships are also marked with governments that denied democratic power to citizens. In contrast to this history, the country is also

Anastasio Somoza Debayle was the second son of Anastasio Somoza Garcia and the last member of the Somoza family to be president of Nicaragua. Somoza Debayle ran a corrupt government and was accused of committing human rights violations. In 1975, the Somoza government launched a violent campaign against a revolutionary group called the Sandinista National Liberation Front.

the first in the Western Hemisphere to have elected a woman, Violeta Chamorro, as president in 1990.

With its checkered political heritage—which, in many respects, is nevertheless fascinating—a number of questions exist today. Where has this twisted path led the country and what political mechanisms are in place today to govern Nicaragua? What protections do citizens have? What relationships exist between Nicaragua and its Central American neighbors and with the United States today? These questions and many more will be explored in this chapter as we seek to understand how Nicaragua's political and cultural heritage have shaped the country's government.

NICARAGUA'S GOVERNMENT TODAY

Politics and government are always changing in societies. Democracies like the United States work to become more perfect unions. This means that the country continually is striving to become a better place for its citizens. In many places this means that the country operates democratically, justly, and in the best interests of the country and its citizens.

The Republic of Nicaragua is a constitutional democracy that has its modern political roots in the constitution of 1987. This constitution was created during the Sandinista era and was later revised in 1995, 2000, and 2005. The Sandinista National Liberation Front (FSLN) is named after rebel leader Augusto César Sandino, who led the Nicaraguan resistance against U.S. occupation in the 1930s. The FSLN is a socialist political party that historically has exercised considerable political power in Nicaragua. The FSLN's role and political impact will be discussed in greater depth later in this chapter.

Attempts to develop a democracy in Nicaragua have often been fraught with difficulties and frustration and hindered by dictatorial leaders. The country has experienced more than its share of rigged elections, political crackdowns, and rampant corruption. There also have been countless assassinations, political massacres, and human rights violations. These are just some of the political problems that have occurred in twentieth-century Nicaraguan politics.

Keeping the power of leaders in check has been a major problem. Dictators have ruled with iron fists, and political opponents have been killed. This history is one of the reasons that the 1995 change to the Sandinista constitution gave more powers and independence to the legislative branch, the system that passes and amends laws. It is also why the country continues to discuss the potential of becoming a parliamentary system. This change would divide the roles of the chief of state and the head of state, powers that reside today with the president. Given the tendency of the executive branch to abuse its powers, the potential change is attractive to many Nicaraguans. Thus, the historical struggle between the executive, legislative, and judicial branches in the country seems to be resulting in new efforts to improve the country's democracy.

EVENTS LEADING UP TO THE CONSTITUTION

The core of a strong democracy is a country's constitution. Some countries treat their constitution with little regard. This situation often presents citizens with a mess of problems and little protection of their political and civil rights. Before 1987 Nicaragua's constitutions frequently fell prey to the dictatorial whims of leaders such as the Somozas, who controlled the government for nearly a half-century.

The Somoza family gained its power in 1927 with the support of the U.S. government, under the condition that the Somozas replace the reign of the U.S. Marines with the *Guardia Nacional* (National Guard). The Somozas continued to control all branches of the government and were known for being corrupt.

Anastasio Somoza Garcia, the son of wealthy coffee planters, was the patriarch of the Somoza dynasty. He began his political career as a governor and diplomat, and rose through the ranks of the National Guard. He became president in 1937 and immediately amended the constitution so that it gave him total control. He then filled key government and military positions with family members and loyal supporters. Although opposition parties continued to exist, the elections were heavily rigged in support of Somoza Garcia's Nationalist Liberation Party. Already a very wealthy man through underhanded deals with various organizations (for example, during World War II, the government confiscated land from Nicaragua's small but wealthy German community and sold the properties at cheap prices to the Somozas), Somoza Garcia had opposition leaders murdered and took control of their properties. During his second term in office, Somoza Garcia was shot by poet Rigoberto López Pérez in León on September 21, 1956.

Somoza Garcia's eldest son, Luis Anastasio Somoza Debayle, succeeded him as president. Although his time as president, from 1956 to 1963, was considered more tolerant than his father's, corruption remained widespread and civil liberties were suppressed. He died of a heart attack at the age of 45 in 1967.

Conservative Anastasio Somoza Debayle, the second son of Anastasio Somoza Garcia, was the second most powerful man in Nicaragua during his brother's presidency. He had been head of the National Guard since 1947 and used his position to make sure that the presidency was held at the end of his brother's term in 1963 by people loyal to his family. Therefore, even though a Somoza was not officially in control of Nicaragua from 1963 to 1967, Luis Somoza still was effectively dictator of the country until his death in 1967. In 1967, Anastasio Somoza Debayle was elected president and served until 1972. Although the law did not allow consecutive terms, he remained the unofficial ruler of the country as head of the National Guard until he was again elected in 1974. Although Luis was a more tolerant ruler than his father, once Anastasio took over in 1967, any opposition to his administration was not tolerated and civil rights were not observed. His administration was highly corrupt, taking money that was meant for the poor after the devastating 1972 earthquake, acquiring industries that were key to rebuilding the nation, and taxing the elite to further its own greed.

Anastasio Somoza Debayle hated the Sandinistas (FSLN), the political party that was founded in 1961 by angry Nicaraguans who were fed up with the Somozas. The Sandinistas are liberal (and according to some, Marxist), and they returned Somoza Debayle's hatred. Somoza Debayle was finally overthrown in 1979, and the FSLN took power with support of the Catholic Church and the United States under President Jimmy Carter. Somoza fled Nicaragua and was assassinated in Paraguay in 1980, ending the reign of the Somoza dynasty.

In 1981, the United States under President Ronald Reagan believed that the FSLN was assisting Cuba in spreading Marxist revolutionary activities to El Salvador and other countries in the region. In response, an effort was made by the United States to subvert the Sandinistas by having the Central Intelligence Agency (CIA) provide funding and military training to Nicaraguan rebel groups that were hostile to the FSLN. They were called *contrarevolucionarios* (counter-revolutionaries), or Contras. The Contras operated out of camps in neighboring Honduras and Costa Rica, engaging in actions that would disrupt the country's economy, such as planting underwater mines in Nicaragua's Corinto Harbor. (This would prevent cargo ships from passing through.)

The United States also placed a trade embargo on the country and, in 1983, helped to fund the Contras by selling arms to Iran and directing the profits to the Contras. This became known as the Iran-Contra Affair, a political scandal that came to light in 1986. Thus, direct intervention in Nicaraguan affairs, such as that discussed in Chapter 3, continued during the second half of the twentieth century.

Founded in 1961 as a revolutionary group committed to socialism and to the defeat of the Somoza government, the Sandinista National Liberation Front, also known as FSLN or the Sandinistas, had the support of students, workers, and peasants. In 1979, the Sandinistas launched offensive attacks from sanctuaries in Costa Rica and Honduras that finally toppled the regime of Anastasio Somoza Debayle.

THE GOVERNMENT OF NICARAGUA

While Nicaragua's constitutional history has not been as stable as other countries, such as the United States and Canada, the constitution still serves as the primary document that establishes basic government institutions and processes. This section will provide an overview of important features of Nicaragua's constitution.

The Legislative Branch

The legislative branch is responsible for making the laws in a country. Laws are one form of public policy that regulate matters controlled by government. Laws at the national level include a number of features, such as defense, health, and the national budget.

Nicaragua has a unicameral (one-house) legislature called the National Assembly. The country had a bicameral (or two-house) legislature until the new constitution was put in place in 1987. The National Assembly has 92 members. Of these members, 90 are elected though proportional representation. This means that representatives are elected in proportion to the number of votes received. Unlike most other countries, two seats are held for specific individuals. One is for the immediate past president and the other is for the individual who received the second largest number of votes in the last presidential election. At the start of 2009, 38 of the seats in the National Assembly were held by the FSLN, 25 by the Constitutional Liberation Party (PLC), and 23 by the Nicaraguan Liberal Alliance (ALN). Members must be Nicaraguan citizens who are at least 21 years old. They are elected for five-year terms.

The National Assembly can pass laws for the country with a simple majority and can also override presidential vetoes with a majority of the quorum. (A quorum is the minimum number of officers needed to conduct business.) It also chooses members of the Supreme Court from a list provided by the president and has the power to consider and approve or reject budgets submitted by the president. Although historically the president held much power in Nicaragua, a recent constitutional revision has greatly strengthened the counterbalancing strength of the National Assembly.

The Executive Branch

The president is the head of the executive branch. It is armed with powers that are provided by the constitution—or often simply seized from citizens or other branches of the government. Nicaragua has a history of a strong executive branch. Limits to these powers have been a relatively new process in the

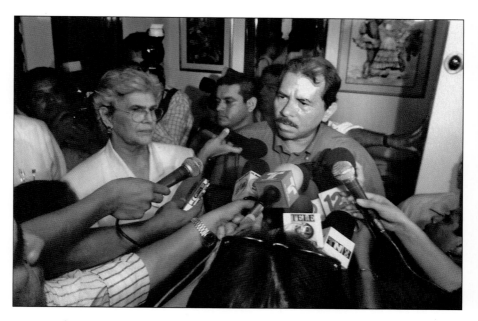

In 1979, the Sandinistas gradually gained control of Nicaragua. In 1985 the group's leader, Daniel Ortega (*right*), became the country's president. In 1990, Ortega was unseated as president by Violeta Chamarro (*left*), the widow of a journalist killed by the Somoza regime. Her appointment made her the first elected female head of government in Latin America. Ortega was elected to a second presidency in 2006.

country. They have not yet withstood the trials of time and a major presidential grab for power. The executive branch is still very powerful, as the checks and balances between the three branches of government are still weighted toward the executive branch. The president has much greater powers than the executives in the United States, Canada, or many other democratic countries. The president even has the power to suspend civil liberties during national emergencies.

The president is directly elected by the citizens for a five-year term on the same ballot as the vice president. Presidents can serve two terms, but they cannot be consecutive. José

Daniel Ortega Saavedra (known as Daniel Ortega), former leader of the Sandinistas, was as of 2010 the president of Nicaragua. He first served as president in 1985, a period characterized by the U.S. support of the Contras. During this period, Ortega was accused of supporting Marxist activities in South America. At the time the country did not have a constitution. Ortega was then defeated in 1990 by Violeta Barrios Torres de Chamorro. Although he remained in the public eye, he was an unsuccessful candidate for president in 1996 and 2001, before he was elected again in 2006.

The Judicial Branch

The highest court in Nicaragua is the Supreme Court. This panel has 16 judges who serve five-year terms. This is different from the U.S. system, in which Supreme Court justices are appointed for life. One problem that arises when justices are appointed for shorter terms is that it can hurt their performance as a judicial body. They end up being more responsive to popular political sentiments than to a long-term commitment to the constitution. Nicaragua has a history of a politicized and corrupt court system that threatens justice and judicial independence in the country. The country's courts are also overburdened with civil cases (disputes between individuals or companies where a monetary award is given to the victim).

The Supreme Court supervises lower courts and also nominates all lower and appellate court judges. (Appellate courts rule on appeals of trial courts.) In addition, the Supreme Court rules on decisions of national importance. As with the legislative branch, however, the powers and influence of an independent judicial branch still pale in comparison to the powers of the executive branch in Nicaragua.

THE COMMUNIST PARTY OF NICARAGUA

Nicaragua has had an active Communist Party for many years. Founded as the Socialist Workers Party in 1967, the party today is known as the Partido Communista de Nicaragua (PCdeN) or the Communist Party of Nicaragua. Although not terribly significant today, the party has had times during which it influenced Nicaragua's political directions. The most significant example occurred in 1990 when it worked with the National Opposition Union to defeat the FSLN. However, PCdeN gained no seats in the 2006 National Assembly elections.

LOCAL GOVERNMENTS

Nicaragua has 15 states, which it calls *departimientos* (departments). The country also has two autonomous (independent) regions, Atlantico Norte (North Atlantic) and Atlantico Sur (South Atlantic). The country is governed by a unitary system, rather than a federal system. This means that all governments in Nicaragua are governed at the national level, which is supreme. In addition to the departments, the country has 153 municipalities. Local governments have gained more power in recent years and are now free to elect many local officials such as mayors.

NICARAGUA'S GOVERNMENT AND ITS CITIZENS

Since Nicaragua has had a turbulent past marked by many strong and dictatorial leaders, the rights of citizens have been frequently violated. According to the U.S. Department of State, such violations include police abuses, a lack of the rule of law, and violations of freedom of speech and the press. Some citizens have even been killed by the country's security forces. Violence has also taken place in particular against women, minorities, and trade union members. Thus, even with freedoms and rights protected in the constitution, the country's government doesn't necessarily respect these rights.

What protections are in the constitution? The following is a list of a few of the freedoms and rights that the constitution says are to be protected:

- The right to freedom, security, and personality

- The right to privacy

- The right to equal protection under the law

- Freedom of conscience, thought, and religion

- Freedom of expression in public or private

- Freedom of movement within the country

- Freedom from random arrest and detention

- The right to not testify against yourself or your spouse

- The right to be considered innocent until proven guilty

- Freedom from torture or cruel and inhumane punishment

- The right to own property

- The right to assemble and get involved in political activity

FOREIGN RELATIONS

After the 1990 election, Nicaragua pursued foreign relations with a more democratic government than experienced under the Sandinistas. Today, the country is active in the region as well as in many international organizations. Nicaragua has an independent foreign policy.

Nicaragua's current relationship with the United States is worth examining because in the past the United States has often been very involved in Nicaraguan affairs. In addition, it provides financial assistance to Nicaragua, which has totaled more than $2 billion since 1990. Presently, the U.S. State Department suggests four goals for Nicaragua. These include the following areas:

- Improving the respect for human rights in Nicaragua

- Developing a free-market economy with a respect for property and intellectual property rights

- Increasing Nicaragua's ability to combat cross-border issues such as trafficking in people, weapons, and drugs

- Reforming the judicial system

In Central America, Nicaragua has been a positive force in recent years. It has been instrumental in settling several heated disputes with and between neighbors. Territorial disputes with Honduras and Colombia have been settled in the International Court at The Hague in the Netherlands, and a water issue between Nicaragua and Costa Rica was also under consideration by the court in 2009. With international organizations like the International Court involved in resolving standing disputes between countries, Nicaragua has spent less on its military.

Nicaragua also belongs to the United Nations and many other related international agencies, including the World Bank, the International Monetary Fund, the World Trade Organization, the United Nations Human Rights Commission, and the World Health Organization. Other international organization ties include the Organization of American States, the Non-aligned Movement, the Central American Common Market, and the International Atomic Energy Commission.

REFLECTING UPON NICARAGUA'S GOVERNMENT

Nicaragua's democracy is still in its infancy. An unusually powerful executive branch still encourages dictatorial tendencies. These tendencies have not yet been weeded out following decades of strong-arm government. Because of this, human rights are still being violated and major problems of corruption and political manipulation are still far too frequent in the judicial system. The country is also the second poorest in the Americas, behind troubled Haiti, and also comes second only to Haiti as the lowest-ranked nation in the Western Hemisphere on the Human Development Index (HDI). Both rankings impose a tremendous challenge for the country's government.

There are, however, several bright spots on Nicaragua's political landscape. The country can take pride in having elected the first female president in the Americas—Violeta Barrios Torres de Chamorro in 1990. In addition, the legislative and judicial branches have become stronger with recent constitutional limits to the powers of the executive branch. The country has also been pressing for demilitarization in the region, an effort that could lead to continuing peaceful relations with neighboring countries.

Nevertheless, the challenge for Nicaragua will be to stick to its constitution. The nation's big test will be to keep checking the power of its hyperactive executive branch. Nicaraguans hope this problem will soon fade from memory. They long for political stability that will lead to economic growth and prosperity for the country and its people.

CHAPTER

6

Nicaragua's Economy

N icaragua's economy has long been in shambles. It is the second weakest in the Western Hemisphere, as measured by several economic indicators. Only Haiti ranks below Nicaragua in such categories as per capita income and per capita gross national product (two categories that will be discussed further in this chapter). In numerous other categories the country also ranks very near the bottom.

In this chapter, you will learn about the highs and lows of Nicaragua's economy. We will begin with an overview of the country's economic conditions and an explanation of why the country is so poor. You will then learn about its various industries and how each sector contributes to the country's economy. Finally, you will learn about Nicaragua's place in the economic world based upon its global linkages.

ECONOMIC OVERVIEW

There are dozens of ways to measure a country's economy and to determine its ranking among the world's nations. Here, only a few such measures are presented. Economic statistics, after all, can and do change very rapidly. Most of those presented here are taken from the *CIA World Factbook* (2009). They are included to help you gain a general understanding of the country's economic condition, rather than to burden you with statistics.

By most measures, if not all, Nicaragua falls within a group of countries called "developing," "less developed," or "Third World." This status is based upon many factors. For example, the gross national product (GNP)—the annual value of all goods and services produced in the country—is $16.79 billion. This figure is meaningless, of course, unless it is placed in some relative context. If you knew that Nicaragua ranks 130 among the world's 228 countries, you could guess that about 60 percent of all nations have a higher GNP. Even more revealing is the fact that Nicaragua has the lowest GNP of any Spanish- or Portuguese-speaking country in the Americas. How does this figure break down on a per capita (per person) basis? Nicaragua's per capita GNP is a slim $2,900, which places it at number 168 among nations, ahead of only Haiti in the Western Hemisphere.

Individual incomes do not fare much better. The average Nicaraguan has an annual income of about $2,400. In the Americas, once again, only impoverished Haitians rank lower in this measure of poverty. But it gets worse! In 2008, the country's inflation rate was nearly 20 percent, one of the highest in the world. What this means for Nicaraguans is 20 percent higher prices, or a 20 percent reduction in how much people can afford to buy. Their meager financial resources simply don't go as far as they would in nearly any other country. In Latin America, only oil-rich Venezuela has a higher rate of inflation.

Due to massive underemployment, low per capita income, and huge debts to other countries, Nicaragua is one of the Western Hemisphere's poorest countries, with 48 percent of the population living below the poverty line. Although the country has made progress toward national economic stability, Nicaragua continues to be dependent on international aid and debt relief. Above, two men look for recyclable garbage on a street in Managua.

Unemployment also is average, running at between 5 and 6 percent. This figure, however, is also relatively meaningless, because nearly half of all Nicaraguans are *under*employed, at 46.5 percent. What this means is that they have one or more jobs but do not hold full-time jobs that allow them to earn an adequate income. The distribution of wealth is another matter of concern. Of the Nicaraguan population, 48 percent lives below the poverty line. The lowest 10 percent of the population possess only 1.4 percent of the nation's capital (money used to make products or provide services). The highest 10 percent hold 41.8 percent of the wealth.

In 2009, Nicaragua's economy suffered along with that of most other countries as a result of the global economic slow-down. Prices for many Nicaraguan exports declined due to the global economic slump. The country's economy also depends quite heavily on international assistance. During the global recession, donors have been much less generous. Because of internal political problems—yes, they continue—foreign investment once again has slowed. Finally, nearly 15 percent of the country's GDP comes from money sent home by Nica-raguans living abroad, and this also has dropped sharply as a result of the global economic hard times.

These are just some of the measures of a country's eco-nomic well-being. There are many others, some that are not attached to a dollar sign. For example, energy consumption, literacy rates, and the number of physicians per capita suggests whether a country is rich or poor. One of the best indicators of a country's well-being is the Human Development Index (HDI). The HDI is based upon life expectancy, literacy, educa-tion, and standards of living for the world's countries. Nicara-gua ranks 124 among the 182 nations included in the survey. Once again, in the Western Hemisphere only Haiti ranks lower than Nicaragua in this detailed measure.

KEYS TO ECONOMIC SUCCESS

Why is Nicaragua such a poor country? Its physical environ-ment is no better or worse, in terms of economic potentials, than that of many or most Latin American nations. There are 19 other American nations that share a similar Spanish colo-nial experience. Colonization cannot be given all the blame. In addition, Nicaraguans do not have extreme cultural differ-ences from most other countries in Latin America. So what went wrong?

Much of the blame falls to the country's long history of seemingly endless turmoil and civil conflict. From the very beginning of Spanish colonization, Nicaragua has been torn between liberal and conservative sides. For a country's economy to be successful, people must work together for the common good of their nation.

When one searches for a key to national prosperity (or poverty), one usually need look no further than to the government. Is the government stable, responsible, and responsive to the needs of its people? As you learned in Chapter 3, Nicaragua has rarely had a responsible democratic government. When a country is poorly governed, both citizens and foreigners are hesitant to invest money that is so desperately needed for development. Corrupt governments care little about their citizens and show little concern for developing public services such as education, health care, and transportation infrastructure.

As a result, Nicaragua has one of the lowest literacy rates and ranks among the poorest countries in terms of public health in Latin America. Only about two-thirds of the adult population can read and write. Many Nicaraguans suffer from health-related issues that sap their energy and make them less able to work, and their life expectancy is one of the lowest in the Western Hemisphere. A healthy and well-educated workforce is essential to the prosperity of a country.

A great number of conditions must come together for a country to enjoy a strong economy. You might think that abundant natural resources are essential, but this is not necessarily true. Many countries, including economic powerhouse Japan, have almost no natural resources or raw materials. What economically strong countries do have, if they are successful, is a government that promotes economic development and growth. A primary way to achieve economic success is to support a capitalist (free market) economy. Such an economy respects work ethic and promotes free and fair competition in the marketplace and workplace. Unfortunately, Nicaragua has a long way to go before catching up with its Latin American neighbors in these vital areas.

Finally, most economically well-developed countries have yet another thing in common. Their economy is based mainly upon the service sector and most of their labor force works in various services as well. Service jobs include positions in such areas as sales, education, health care, transportation, tourism, or communications. In Nicaragua, only about half of the labor force is engaged in providing services. Slightly less than 60 percent of the country's GDP comes from service-related economic activities. By comparison, about 80 percent of the workforce in the United States and other developed countries is engaged in service-related industries. Let's look at the various sectors of Nicaragua's economy.

PRIMARY INDUSTRIES

Primary industries are those in which basic natural resources—soils, minerals, forests, and other natural elements—are exploited for economic gain. Once they are extracted, they become raw materials used in the processing of products in the primary sector of the economy. Major activities in the primary economic sector include: agriculture (farming and ranching); mineral products (mining, quarrying, and the extraction of petroleum and natural gas); forestry (logging and the gathering of forest products such as nuts and other products); and fishing (sport and commercial, including shellfish and crustaceans).

In most developed countries, the primary sector of the economy involves very few people. In the United States, for example, only about 0.6 percent of the workforce is engaged in primary industries. In Nicaragua, that figure is about 30 percent. As a general rule, primary industry employment pays relatively low wages. This is because these jobs require less education, training, and skills than do the jobs within the secondary and tertiary economic sectors.

Agriculture

Agriculture—raising livestock and growing crops—has played an important role in Nicaragua's economy since the earliest years of Spanish settlement. It continues to be important today, but at a much lower level of importance. Historically, beef and animal products such as leather and hides were Nicaragua's leading agricultural export. Livestock were raised on large ranches located mainly in the central and western regions of the country.

Traditionally, the major export crops have been coffee and cotton, both raised on plantations. Sugarcane also is an important plantation crop. During recent years tobacco, sesame (for seeds and oil), and palm oil have become significant export products. Surprisingly, this Central American nation has never produced bananas as a major crop, as some of its neighbors do. Other agricultural crops include cotton, rice, corn, and beans. Animal products include beef, veal, pork, poultry, and dairy items.

During recent decades, Nicaraguan agriculture has sharply declined in importance. In the 1970s, nearly two-thirds of the workforce was engaged in farming or ranching. Agriculture contributed about 40 percent of the country's GDP. A whopping 80 percent of export income was generated by agricultural exports. Today, about 30 percent of the Nicaraguan workforce is engaged in this sector of the economy, and agriculture contributes only about 17 percent of the country's gross domestic product.

A number of factors contributed to the huge drop in agricultural production. The chief factor was the political turmoil and civil conflict the country experienced during the 1980s. During this period, a great deal of land went out of production. Investment in agriculture plummeted because of the uncertain political and economic environment. Plant diseases, droughts and floods, and the growth of other economic sectors also took a toll on agriculture and its importance to the nation's economy.

Until the Sandinista revolution, agriculture was a significant part of the Nicaraguan economy. Agricultural production declined in the 1980s due to a decrease in investments from private industries, devastation from hurricanes and droughts, and intentional destruction of farms and plants by the guerrilla group. Nontraditional export crops like tobacco (*shown above*) were the only products that showed growth.

Mineral Industries

It was gold, you will recall, that some believe attracted Columbus's attention to the Amerique Mountains and may have resulted in the name "America" for the western continents. From the earliest period of Spanish settlement in Nicaragua, gold mining has been an important economic activity. In the past, small deposits of copper, molybdenum, and tungsten have been mined. The country also has ample reserves of stone, gravel, sand, and clay, all of which are used in construction. Gold, however, continues to contribute about 87 percent of the total value of Nicaragua's mineral production. Even so, the value of all mining combined contributes only a fraction of one percent of the country's GDP.

Nicaragua's economy is severely handicapped by the country's lack of fossil fuels. There are no deposits of coal, petroleum, or natural gas. During recent years, there has been some offshore exploration for petroleum and natural gas in both the Caribbean and Pacific waters. As of 2010, however, no discoveries had been made.

Forestry

Much of central and eastern Nicaragua is heavily forested. Commercial logging, however, has never been a significant contributor to the country's GDP. One problem is that many tree species within the tropical rain forest are softwoods that have little commercial value. Valued hardwood species, such as mahogany and teak, are widely scattered about the forest, rather than in homogeneous groups. This makes finding and harvesting them very difficult.

In many places, forests have been cleared to create farmland. In fact, since the 1950s, more than 60 percent of Nicaragua's woodlands have been destroyed.

At the current rate of deforestation, some estimates suggest that the remaining forests will be gone by 2020. As a result, the government has stepped in. It wants to make lumber resources sustainable, that is, able to be maintained at a certain level over the long term. Today, Nicaragua has about 10,000 square miles (25,900 sq km) of forest plantations, or tree farms. They produce wood that contributes about $3.5 million annually to the country's GDP.

Fisheries

Nicaragua is rich in aquatic resources. Marine life, including fish, shellfish, and crustaceans, abound in the waters of the Pacific and the Caribbean. The country's two large lakes and many rivers also teem with fish, including, you will recall, the freshwater sharks in Lake Nicaragua and the San Juan River. Fish account for only a tiny fraction of Nicaragua's export income. Many residents, however, depend upon fishing as a major source of their food supply. Sport fishing has also become very popular, attracting tourists to both saltwater and freshwater bodies. Prized species include marlin, rainbow bass, sailfish, snook, tarpon, sailfish, and yellowfin tuna. Shrimp and lobsters are also of economic importance.

Today, Nicaragua's most important marine export is farmed shrimp. In fact, farmed shrimp contribute more than 40 percent of the country's total fishing industry. Most of this development is found along the northwest coast, where 80 percent of the country's shrimp farms are found in the Real Estuary near Chinandega. The industry has grown rapidly, resulting in a current annual average production of more than 50 million pounds (24 million kg) of the tasty morsels.

SECONDARY INDUSTRIES

Secondary industries are those that create finished products from natural resources and raw materials. They include manufacturing, construction, and energy-producing industries. Stereotypically, this sector has involved blue-collar laborers working in factories or at construction sites. In economically developed countries, this was the major economic sector until sometime in the mid-1900s. It remains an important activity in many economically developing countries. In Nicaragua, 19 percent of the labor force is engaged in secondary industries, which produce about 25 percent of the country's GDP.

As you can imagine, all Nicaraguan industries suffered greatly during the long period of civil strife. Prior to the early 1980s, nearly three-fourths of the country's industry was related in some way to agriculture. They either produced items such as fertilizer or processed agricultural products such as tobacco. By 1990, however, Nicaragua's secondary industries were struggling. The Contra-Sandinista hostilities had discouraged both foreign and domestic investment in the country's economy. Many factories and production methods were behind the times, as was the equipment. Much of the country's industry-supporting infrastructure, such as power supply and transportation facilities, was in ruin. Labor unrest was widespread.

As is true of manufacturing in most developing countries, industries tend to be quite basic. They produce items requiring minimal skilled labor and little advanced technology. Most products are low-cost items or materials upon which local people depend. In Nicaragua, they include food processing, tobacco, and beverages such as beer and soft drinks. Textiles, clothing, and footwear are also manufactured, as are various wood products. Some machinery, various metal products, and chemicals are also manufactured.

The Booming Textile Industry

There is one bright spot in an otherwise rather dark and dreary Nicaraguan manufacturing economy. During recent years, the textile industry has experienced tremendous growth. In 2008, more than 70 textile and apparel companies were doing business in the country. The value of these exports was approaching $1 billion in 2009. According to PRONicaragua, an agency that promotes foreign investment in Nicaragua, the country's apparel companies currently manufacture products for such world-renowned brands as Polo, Ralph Lauren, Liz Claiborne, Phillips-Van Heusen, Wrangler, Cintas, Dickies, and Hanes. They also make clothing for major retailers including Target, JCPenney, Walmart, Sears, Gap, and Kohl's. Denim production is a specialty. If you have blue jeans, the odds are good that they were made in Nicaragua. You might want to check the label.

Many industries complement one another—that is, they provide services and materials upon which another industry depends. Think for a moment of the automobile industry. How many different manufacturers supply items that go into the making of motor vehicles? It is the same with textiles and clothing. According to PRONicaragua, firms that complement the textile industry include companies that offer services in embroidery, industrial laundry, dying and finishing, cutting rooms, labels, thread, and packaging materials. Then, of course, there are the firms that supply energy to factories, transport raw materials and finished products, provide financing, and so forth.

Construction

Much of Nicaragua's infrastructure has been destroyed repeatedly by earthquakes, hurricanes, floods, or warfare. Because of such recent losses, one would think that the country would be a hotbed of construction activity. Unfortunately, poverty and uncertainty stand in the way of a much-needed construction boom.

Energy

An adequate supply of energy is essential to the economy and the well-being of citizens in any country. According to many economists, geographers, and energy experts, the per capita consumption of energy is the single most valid indicator of a country's cultural development and economic growth. In order for this to happen, of course, energy must be available. This is a problem for Nicaragua. It lacks coal, petroleum, and natural gas resources. In fact, the need to import petroleum is a major contributor to the country's staggering trade imbalance.

During the civil war, Nicaragua's power grid—the country's infrastructure to distribute electricity—was damaged extensively. Restoration has been slow, with most of the effort being directed toward providing electrical power to cities. As recently as 2007, however, Nicaragua was unable to meet the demand for electricity. In fact, the public needed 16 percent more energy than the power grid could supply. This shortage resulted in widespread urban power blackouts.

About 80 percent of Nicaragua's electrical energy is generated by petroleum-powered plants. Most of the country's
petroleum (including fuel for vehicles and other uses) is
imported from Mexico and Venezuela. Currently, the country
is attempting to reduce its dependence on costly foreign oil.
Ambitious plans are underway to expand production from
renewable energy sources. These include an increase in hydroelectric energy, geothermal installations, cane-burning plants,
and even wind power. Seven such projects are scheduled to
come online by 2011.

Although Nicaragua has great energy-producing potential,
most Nicaraguans endure what is described as a "daily battle
for energy survival." The country's only oil refinery experiences
constant technical problems and shutdowns. In 2008, there was
a plan that had financial support to build the largest oil refinery
in Central America in Nicaragua. It was to be a joint venture
between the Venezuelan and Nicaraguan government-owned
petroleum agencies. Unfortunately, as so often happens in
developing countries, the venture became the focus of a gigan-
tic scandal: All but $1 million of the $250 million earmarked
for building the refinery disappeared!

TERTIARY (SERVICE) INDUSTRIES

In 2008, between 55 and 60 percent of the Nicaraguan gross
domestic product was generated by the economy's tertiary
sector, or service sector. This is one of the lowest percentages
in all of Latin America. The proportion of a country's working population engaged in providing services is a key factor in
determining its level of economic development. In the United
States and most other developed countries, for example, at least
80 percent of the workforce is engaged in the tertiary sector of
the economy.

Service industries are those that in some way serve the
public. The sector includes wholesale and retail sales, all kinds
of transportation, and communications. Health care, clerical

services, education, law, banking, and insurance also are service-related activities. So are entertainment, restaurants, lodging, and tourism. As you can imagine, when a country is at war
with itself, most if not all of these industries suffer. Certainly
that was the case in Nicaragua. Assuming the country's political climate stabilizes and both foreign and domestic investment
are encouraged, Nicaragua's service sector should boom.

Transportation

Transportation, economic development, and human well-being
go hand in hand. If a country's economy is strong, it can afford
to build a solid transportation network. On the other hand, a
well-developed transportation network contributes greatly to
economic development. If an economy is growing and citizens
can travel with ease, they should prosper. In Nicaragua, transportation facilities are quite inadequate. Amazingly, it is the
only mainland Latin American country that has not a mile of
railroad linkages. There is only one international airport, which
is located in Managua.

Only 1,429 miles (2,299 km) of the country's roads are
paved, or about 12 percent of the total. Many of the unim-
proved roadways are impassable during parts of the year. Nearly
all roadways are in the densely settled western part of the country. Many areas of eastern Nicaragua are inaccessible by road.
Corinto and San Juan del Sur are important seaports on the
Pacific coast. Bluefields is the leading Caribbean port, but its
role is minimized by its distance from the country's major population centers. Clearly, improving Nicaragua's transportation
facilities and linkages poses a huge challenge for the country's
leaders in coming decades.

Tourism

One potentially bright spot in Nicaragua's otherwise rather dismal economy is the tourism industry. With the end of domestic

Tourism is the second-largest industry in Nicaragua. Granada's beautiful colonial architecture, rich history, and fine museums have made it the preferred spot in the country for tourists from the United States, Central and South America, and Europe. Pictured is the Cathedral of Granada, which was built in the neoclassical style.

hostilities and the dawn of the twenty-first century, tourism has shown remarkable promise, growing an average of 10 to nearly 20 percent annually. Today, it is the second-largest contributor to the country's gross domestic product. When tourism prospers, so do other sectors of the economy. Tourist facilities must be built, giving a boost to the construction industry. Various tourist-related businesses such as vehicle rental, lodging accommodations, and restaurants prosper. Financial institutions benefit. And, of course, the tourism industry generates thousands of jobs.

There are many things that can attract tourists to Nicaragua. Certainly the country has much to offer in terms of scenery. Attractions include its rugged volcanic peaks and huge lakes. Beautiful beaches are a draw, as are the mysterious rain forests with their fascinating flora and fauna. So are the country's friendly people and their culture. Many tourists are attracted by the magnificent examples of colonial architecture and other historical sights in cities such as Granada and León. Since 2000, San Juan del Sur, located on the Pacific coast near the Costa Rican border, has become an important cruise ship stopover. About 50,000 tourists visit the country through this port each year.

One advantage that Nicaraguan tourism can build upon is the wide variety of experiences that the country can offer tourists. It offers mountain hiking, ocean surfing and snorkeling, saltwater and freshwater fishing, urban experiences, and lounging on the beach. Visitors can also visit a coffee *finca* (farm), spend the night, and learn about coffee production and processing.

The greatest opportunity for growth may be with ecotourism. Ecotourists want to experience nature in the raw and culture in its traditional state. This kind of tourism emphasizes local culture, customs, cuisine, and traditions. Ecotourists want to wander the rain forest or hike mountain trails. They seek a kind of adventure that is not found in urban hotels, souvenir shops, upscale restaurants, and other common tourist attractions. Nicaragua has taken steps to actively encourage the development of this sector of the tourism industry. The country has set aside nearly 80 environmentally protected areas that cover about 20 percent of its total area.

FOREIGN TRADE

Nicaragua imports many more goods than it exports. This has contributed to an annual trade deficit of more than $2 billion. This imbalance imposes a condition that further erodes the country's economy.

Imports include petroleum products, raw materials, consumer goods, and machinery and equipment including automobiles. The United States is the leading producer of imported items, amounting to about 21 percent of the total value. Venezuela and Mexico, both of which supply the country with petroleum, are close behind. Exports include textiles and clothing, several seafood items including shrimp and lobster, and small amounts of gold. Agricultural products include beef, coffee, tobacco, sugar, and peanuts. Nearly a third of all exports go to the United States, with most of the rest going to Mexico and Nicaragua's Central American neighbors.

Since 2006, Nicaragua has benefited from its membership in the U.S.-Dominican Republic-Central America Free Trade Agreement (CAFTA-DR). This agreement, similar in nature to the North American Free Trade Agreement (NAFTA), reduces barriers to trade between countries. It has expanded trade opportunities for many items, including manufactured goods and agricultural products.

Nicaragua remains at or near the bottom of Latin American countries in many, if not most, economic categories. In the Western Hemisphere, only Haiti has a more dismal overall economic condition. Nicaragua has a number of hurdles to jump before it can begin to develop its potential. Of greatest importance, it must achieve long-term political stability. If this is accomplished, both Nicaraguans and foreign interests will begin to invest economically in the country's future. If recoverable petroleum deposits are found in the country's territorial waters, this will help to solve the country's critical energy problem. If oil is not found, alternative energy sources must be further developed. Wind, solar, geothermal, hydro, and biotic sources are abundant and can be harnessed. Finally, the transportation infrastructure must be further developed. Nicaragua faces many economic challenges. Hopefully the progress experienced during the dawn of the twenty-first century will continue.

CHAPTER

7

Regions of Nicaragua

I n many respects, there are three "Nicaraguas," each of which is markedly different from the other two. The extensive, remote, and sparsely populated tropical Eastern Lowlands seem a world apart from the heavily populated Western Lowlands. Sandwiched between these two vastly different worlds are the Central Highlands. Until recently, no road linked east and west, although a single poorly maintained dirt road does exist today. The resulting isolation has helped to maintain the "different worlds" feeling. In this chapter, you will visit Nicaragua's three major geographic regions: the Eastern Lowlands, the Central Highlands, and the Pacific Lowlands.

EASTERN LOWLANDS (ATLANTIC, CARIBBEAN, MISKITO)

Between the Central Highlands and the Caribbean coast is a low-lying belt of steaming tropical lowlands. The region is recognized by several names, including Eastern Lowlands, Atlantic Lowlands, Caribbean Lowlands, and Miskito Lowlands or Miskito Coast. Physically, the region is quite isolated from the remainder of Nicaragua. In fact, until recently it has been largely outside the realm of effective national control. In other words, it was hard to reach and communications were poorly developed. Politically, it was difficult—if not impossible—for the government, located in the west, to be in charge of the remote region. Physically and culturally, the people of the Eastern Lowlands resemble those of the Caribbean islands much more than they do Latin Americans. For the most part, their history, language, religion, diet, and economic activity set them far apart from other Nicaraguans.

Physical Environment

The Eastern Lowlands were formed when streams deposited silt eroded from the interior highlands. Over several million years, these deposits of silt reached a depth of several thousand feet. Unlike the Pacific coastal zone, the Caribbean coast is very irregular. There are many river deltas that continue to deposit silt into the sea. As the silt is reworked by waves and currents, it forms barrier islands, beach ridges, and other low-lying features. A number of lagoons also dot the coastal region.

Eastern Nicaragua lies in the path of the very constant northeast trade winds. As the winds sweep across the warm Caribbean, they pick up huge amounts of moisture. Upon reaching land, much of the moisture is released, making the region the rainiest in all of Central America. Much of the coastal region receives 100 inches (250 cm) or more rainfall each year, with some locations receiving as much as 250 inches (635 cm). Temperatures remain consistently high throughout the year; so does the humidity, which makes conditions extremely muggy. During the summer, which is the wetter season, the coastal zone is vulnerable to severe flooding from

normal rainfall. Occasional hurricanes add to the region's environmental misery.

The Miskito rain forest, much of which covers the Eastern
Lowlands, occupies an area of more than 7,700 square miles
(20,000 sq km), nearly the size of New Jersey. It is the second
largest rain forest in the Americas, exceeded in area only by the
vast Amazon rain forest. Two reserves, Bosawás in the north
and Indio Maiz in the south, have been established to preserve
this national treasure. The forest is rich in wildlife and includes
hundreds of species of birds, insects, various reptiles (some of
which are deadly), monkeys, anteaters, and strange-looking
tapirs. Not all of the vegetation cover is rain forest. The lowland
also has an area of pine-dotted savanna grasslands that extend
some 300 miles (nearly 500 km) along the coastal zone north
of Bluefields.

Human Geography

Long before the arrival of the Spaniards, many Amerindians
practiced a form of slash-and-burn shifting cultivation. Vegetation was cleared by cutting and then burning plant cover before
fields were planted. On the fertile stream-deposited soil, yields
were low but much higher than those in the Central Highlands.
Unlike in the interior, field clearings did not have to be moved
every few years because of worn-out soil. Today, a few Amerindians continue to practice this type of subsistence farming.

As early as the sixteenth century, English and Dutch pirates
frequented the Caribbean coastal zone. They found it to be an
ideal location from which to strike gold-laden Spanish ships.
The area was also of interest to Jamaicans and other British-
Caribbean peoples. By 1678 the British had seized the region, a
grip they held until late in the nineteenth century when Nicaragua regained control of the Miskito Coast. The British also had
many holdings in the Caribbean. This helps to explain many of
the population's unique features. For example, the population

For centuries the Miskito rain forest was an impenetrable jungle, protecting the Miskito people from conquest. Today, Central America's largest rain forest is shrinking rapidly, threatened by new roads, deforestation, and mining companies.

includes many blacks, English is widely spoken, and religions other than Roman Catholicism are widely practiced.

Bluefields is Nicaragua's oldest city facing the Caribbean. It was settled in 1602. Today, it has a metropolitan area population of about 50,000, making it the region's largest urban center and Nicaragua's major Caribbean port. As of 2010, however, no road linked Bluefields with the remainder of the country. All travel and shipping of goods must be made by water, which is slow, or by air, which is very costly. Access to western Nicaragua can be gained by boat up the San Juan River and into Lake Nicaragua. Major exports from the region include tropical hardwoods and seafood, such as shrimp and lobsters. The city has experienced a direct hit by a hurricane once every 35 years on average. In 1988, Bluefields was all but destroyed by Hurricane Joan, but it was rebuilt.

The Miskito Indian's Turtle Dilemma

The coastal-dwelling Miskito Indians long practiced a subsistence economy. They lived off the land and water, and everything they produced, caught, or gathered was for their own consumption. By raising crops and harvesting marine resources (including green turtles during part of the year), the Miskito fared well for centuries, if not millennia.

During the mid-1900s, however, things began to change. Arrival of the air age and faster water transportation boosted travel to and from the coast. Eventually, a road linked the coastal town of Puerto Cabezas to the rest of the country. As a result, the region's people began to have increased contact with the outside world. New ideas and goods began to reach the Miskito and others living along the coast. This, in turn, resulted in an increased awareness of "outside" ways of living.

The Miskito culture began to change. Instead of practicing a traditional folk lifestyle based upon self-sufficiency, many Miskito yearned for a more "modern" way of life. In the past, they either provided for themselves or traded for goods and services provided by others. Now, however, they were being drawn into a cash economy. They had to earn an income in order to pay for goods and services obtained. Little did the Miskito know that their life and environment were about to change in dramatic ways.

A lively outside commercial market existed for green turtles, including their shells, leather, and meat. In order to profit from this demand, companies moved in to buy, process, and

Fishing for marine turtles dates back to ancient times. Miskitos once hunted green turtles for food but turned to hunting them for economic reasons once large quantities of turtle meat was exported internationally. A decline in the green turtle populations has led to turtle fishing returning to local consumption.

export turtle products. To take advantage of the new economic opportunity, the Miskito began to hunt turtles year-round, for which they were paid cash and even extended credit. As more people became involved in turtle hunting, farms were abandoned and other means of subsistence began to decline. Economically, the Miskito became almost totally dependent upon catching and selling turtles. And, of course, they became increasingly dependent upon cash and the things that it could buy. It was not long before their old ways of surviving were but a faded memory.

Soon, however, their fortunes began to change, and to change drastically. Because companies had extended credit, many Miskito found themselves deeply in debt. The answer, of course, was to catch more turtles. This resulted in a catastrophic decline in the green turtle population. With the turtle population decimated and their subsistence economy collapsed, the Miskito faced disaster. Many observers even thought that they would disappear as a people, or at least vanish as a culture.

But the Miskito were not yet down and out. In 1991, with the help of the Nicaraguan government, they created a protected area called the Cayos Miskitos and Franja Costera Marine Biological Reserve. The reserve covers an area of slightly more than 5,000 square miles (13,000 sq km). It includes an extensive coastal area, many offshore keys (islands), and nearly 40 Miskito communities. Today, the Miskito continue to struggle with outsiders over control of their lands and resources. But with government assistance, it appears that the Miskito people are benefiting from the project. Turtle and other marine resource populations have rebounded. On the reserve, conservation measures have been implemented. And of greatest importance, today the Miskito culture is thriving once again.

CENTRAL HIGHLANDS

The Central Highlands reach southward from Honduras and continue into Costa Rica and beyond. They cover a large portion of Nicaragua, sandwiched between the Eastern and Western Lowlands. Geologically, the Central Highlands are part of a much larger continuous mountain chain that extends from Alaska to the southern tip of South America.

Physical Environment

In some respects, the Central Highlands offer Nicaragua's most pleasant physical conditions. The region has pleasant scenery, fertile valleys with rich soils, and, of greatest importance, cooler temperatures than those that exist elsewhere. Major ranges include the Cordillera Isabella in the north and Cordillera Chontaleña in the south. Near the border with Honduras, Pico Mogoton reaches an elevation of 6,909 feet (2,107 m), the highest point in Nicaragua.

The highlands slope gently to the east and dip steeply to the west. As a result, many large streams flow year-round from the highlands eastward into the Caribbean. They have created a rugged terrain of sharply defined ridges and valleys on the eastern flank. Fewer streams flow westward. Those that do are short, have a steep drop, and may not flow at all during the dry winter season.

Temperatures, on average, decrease by about 3.5°F with every 1,000-foot increase in elevation (0.65°C per 100 m). Although some mountains stand about 7,000 feet (2,134 m) above sea level, most settlement and agricultural activity occurs at elevations between 2,000 and 4,000 feet (600 to 1200 m). Here, temperatures are about 7°F to 14°F (1.3°C to 2.6°C) cooler than in the Eastern and Western Lowlands. As winds off the Caribbean sweep up the eastward-facing mountain slopes, they drop their moisture in huge amounts. As they pass across the mountain crests, however, they are much drier—a condition called the rainshadow effect. Tropical rain forest dominates the eastern slopes, whereas oak and pine forests are common in the drier west.

Human Geography

When the Spaniards arrived in what is now Nicaragua, they found the Central Highlands inhabited by scattered groups of indigenous people. They practiced slash-and-burn agriculture and hunted, and some fished.

European settlement of the highlands came relatively late. Coffee was introduced into Nicaragua in the 1850s by German immigrants. Planters found an ideal environment for the valuable crop in the fertile soils and cooler temperatures of the uplands. Coffee has been the agricultural mainstay of the region for well over a century. Spaniards also discovered gold in the mid-nineteenth century. This, too, encouraged settlement in the highlands. (Could this find have been the long-lost source of gold from the "Amerique" mountains to which Columbus referred?) For more than a century, coffee and gold have been the primary products of the highland region.

Matagalpa, with a population of about 110,000, is the largest city in the Central Highlands and one of Nicaragua's most important urban centers. It is located at an elevation of about 2,300 feet (700 m), resulting in very pleasant year-round temperatures. In fact, the city is nicknamed the "Land of Eternal Spring" because of its mild climate. Matagalpa's other nickname is "Pearl of the North." It is economically prosperous and continues to show a noticeable northern European cultural imprint. This is largely the result of the lingering cultural influence of the some 120 German families who settled in the region more than a century ago.

Matagalpa Province is the second-best developed region economically in all of Nicaragua, trailing only Managua Province. Its economy is well diversified. There are more than a dozen major agricultural crops produced, including many fruits, vegetables, and flowers. Coffee remains far and away the leading export crop. Beef and milk are also produced. There is also some light manufacturing, and gold continues to be mined in the region. During recent years, tourism has become increasingly important. The area has many popular resorts, and its mountains attract a growing number of visitors, including ecotourists.

Between Matagalpa and the border with Honduras are a number of thriving communities. Many of them are linked by the Pan-American Highway, the roadway artery that stretches from northern North America to the southern tip of South America. The largest community is Estelí, with a population of about 110,000. The city is located in an ideal environment for growing cigar tobacco. Politics in a distant land played an important role in boosting this part of Estelí's economy. After the Cuban Revolution in 1959, the United States banned the import of Cuban cigars. Many Cuban cigarmakers fled the country and settled in Estelí, making it one of the world's most important cigar-making centers. Because of its location on the Pan-American Highway, splendid scenery, and close proximity to a half dozen natural reserves, the city has also become a major tourist center.

Jinotega, a city of about 50,000, is located in an area that produces about 80 percent of Nicaragua's coffee. The Department of Jinotega is the most war-torn area of the country. During the twentieth century, various rebel forces fought countless battles in the region, causing widespread destruction and disruption. Recovery has been slow, but today the city and surrounding area are once again bustling.

PACIFIC (WESTERN) LOWLANDS

The Pacific Lowlands region is Nicaragua's heart and soul. It offers an environment—physically, culturally, and historically—that is much different than that found elsewhere in the country.

Physical Geography

Physically, the Pacific Lowlands stand apart from the rest of Nicaragua in several important ways. Much of this region occupies a geologic rift—narrow depression created by downward movement of Earth's crust. The Gulf of Fonseca, Lake Managua, and Lake Nicaragua occupy low portions of the rift valley. A distance of only 12 miles (19 km) and a relatively low elevation separate the southwestern shore of Lake Nicaragua and the Pacific Ocean. On several occasions, this route (including the San Juan River) was considered as a site for the construction of a canal across the isthmus.

The region is also studded with more than 20 volcanoes, many of which remain active. Most of the volcanoes are located along a line that extends from Lake Nicaragua northward to the Gulf of Fonseca. Some volcanoes erupt violently. Mount Cosiguina is a volcano located on the far northwestern tip of Nicaragua. In 1835 it erupted with such violence that the sky became dark within a radius of 35 miles (56 km). Dust from the explosion fell on the island of Jamaica, located 700 miles (1,125 km) away. Volcanic eruptions can be beneficial, however, despite their destructive force. Their ash, in time, weathers into extremely fertile soil.

Another way in which the region differs physically from the rest of Nicaragua is that it experiences numerous and often severe earthquakes. The Pacific Lowlands receive several hundred such shocks each year. Most are hardly noticeable, but some have been extremely destructive. Managua, for example, has been almost totally destroyed on two occasions, once in 1931 and again in 1972. It was rebuilt each time on its original site, right on the fault line!

The Pacific Lowlands also have a climate and ecosystem that are much different from conditions found elsewhere in Nicaragua. Because it is on the "rainshadow" (downwind) side of the Central Highlands, the area is relatively dry. Rainfall is seasonal, experiencing a summer peak and a relatively dry winter. Depending upon location, annual precipitation varies from slightly under 30 inches to around 60 inches (700 to 1,500 mm). In the hot, tropical climate, a lot of moisture is lost to evaporation. As a result, dry scrub woodland covers much of the area and many crops are irrigated.

Human Geography

It was in the Pacific Lowlands that the first Spanish explorers and indigenous people came into permanent contact. It was here that Spaniards first sank permanent roots into the mainland of the Americas, with the founding of Granada in 1524. Today, the region is home to most Nicaraguans and is the country's most productive economic area.

The region's low plains and valleys have very fertile soils that have been enriched with layers of volcanic ash. Much of the land is cultivated. For centuries, the area has produced bumper crops of sugarcane and cotton, the region's two chief commercial crops. Livestock ranching also has a long and productive history here.

About three of every four Nicaraguans live in the Pacific Lowlands region. As a result, the region supports the country's highest population density and greatest concentration of urban areas. An understanding of the Pacific Lowlands can best be gained by visiting the region's major cities.

Managua

From the dawn of Spanish settlement, squabbling between residents of conservative Granada and liberal León kept Nicaragua in constant turmoil. The country's capital shifted between the two cities, depending upon who held political power. By the mid-1850s, Nicaraguans were fed up with the bickering. They founded a new capital city, Managua, which became the seat of government in 1858.

Managua is what geographers call a primate city, which means the leading city in a region. With a population approaching 2 million in the metropolitan area, it is the nation's largest city by a wide margin. It is also the country's capital, its major economic and social center, and Nicaragua's primary

Managua, the capital of Nicaragua, is the country's main economic, political, cultural, commercial, and industrial center. Most of the country's multinational corporations are housed here. In 2007, after a major literacy campaign, Managua was declared the first capital city in Central America to overcome illiteracy.

transportation and communications hub. The country's only international airport is also located in Managua. The booming metropolitan area is home to a majority of Nicaraguan industries. It bustles with services, including regional and international trade and commerce activities. Managua takes great pride in the fact that in 2007 it was recognized as being the first major city in Central America to achieve 100 percent literacy of its population.

Nonetheless, there is a downside to Managua. Because it was founded in the mid-nineteenth century, the city has no colonial history to offer. In fact, having been almost destroyed by earthquakes twice during the twentieth century, very little in the city is of historical interest. Few tourists who visit Nicaragua are attracted to the sprawling capital city. Although Managua is a modern city in every respect, don't expect to see towering skyscrapers if you visit. Scientists predict that a major earthquake will strike Managua at least once every half-century.

León

Liberal León is Nicaragua's second-largest city, with a population approaching 200,000. It is also a major historical, cultural, and regional economic center. The city offers many museums, historic sites, and splendid examples of colonial homes, churches, and other structures. It is said to have more churches and cathedrals per capita than any other city in Nicaragua. When Nicaragua gained its independence, León became the capital, although this role occasionally shifted between the city and Granada. The city is recognized as the country's intellectual center. It is also the original home of the Autonomous National University of Nicaragua, established in 1813. Today, however, the main campus and most students are in Managua.

Economically, León is now struggling. It continues to be a regional industrial and commercial center, but its national importance has declined. The region also supports livestock grazing and crop agriculture that includes sugarcane, as well as peanuts, plantains, sorghum, and corn, most of which is grown for domestic consumption.

Granada

Conservative Granada is located on the shore of Lake Nicaragua. With an estimated population of about 110,000, it is Nicaragua's fourth-largest city. Historically, Granada is the country's crowning gem. The city was founded in 1524 by Francisco Hernández de Córdoba. Long seen as a political and regional economic center, today Granada draws thousands of tourists. Many visitors are attracted by the charming Spanish colonial architecture. Others come to enjoy its lakeside beaches and nearby scenic sites, which include spectacular volcanic Ometepe Island in Lake Nicaragua.

Masaya

Masaya is a city of about 125,000 people strategically located midway between Managua and Granada. The city and surrounding region still retain a charming hint of native cultural folkways. A major tourist attraction is the old cultural market. There, one can find many small shops that offer a wide variety of native crafts and other items traditional to the region. In 1989, Masaya was declared the "Cultural Legacy of the Nation" and a year later the "Capital of National Folklore." Masaya Volcano National Park, the country's first national park, lies just a few miles from the city. A road winds up the volcano to its still active (but safe) crater.

Chinandega

Chinandega is Nicaragua's most northwestern city, located close to the border with Honduras. With a population of about 125,000, it is a regional administrative and agricultural center. Sugarcane is the major crop, although other crops, including peanuts and wheat, are grown. The city also produces a liquor that has earned an international reputation for quality.

San Juan del Sur

Although relatively small, with a population of only about 40,000, San Juan del Sur has one major advantage—it is located on the Pacific coast. The city offers beautiful beaches, sport fishing, snorkeling, surfing, and magnificent scenery. During recent decades it has become Nicaragua's major coastal tourist destination.

CHAPTER

8

Nicaragua Looks Ahead

When gazing into a geographical crystal ball in an attempt to visualize Nicaragua's future, all one sees are question marks—many of them. Some things can be predicted with a degree of certainty, but others are difficult, if not impossible, to foretell. All we can do is hope for the best for the country and its nearly 6 million people. If there is any truth to the wisdom that "the past introduces the present (and the future)," there would appear to be little room for optimism. It is oversimplistic to suggest that only time will tell, but in the case of Nicaragua, that cliché rings true.

In terms of its physical geography, looking ahead is rather easy. It is absolutely certain that devastating earthquakes, violent volcanic eruptions, and vicious hurricanes will continue to strike. When and where they will unleash their destructive and often deadly force is unknown. Nature's wrath will also be experienced with periodic withering droughts interspersed with torrential floods in some parts of the country.

On the positive side, forests that once were disappearing rapidly are now being restored. The country has taken an active role in placing huge chunks of land in protected reserves and parks. Endangered animal life, including green turtles, is now protected. Nicaraguans recognize the importance of their natural environment. They now see it as a valuable national treasure, rather than something to use and abuse without regard for the future.

Nicaragua must overcome the issues that historically have caused conflicts and which, on countless occasions, have sharply divided the country. There have been painfully few decades during which bitter dissention has not sapped the country's energy and blocked its potential. In Nicaragua, the seeds of conflict are never far from the surface and can sprout at a moment's notice. One can only wonder when Nicaraguans will simply tire of conflict and say, "Enough!"

Nicaragua's population also offers many challenges. The population is growing at a full half percent higher than the world average. One-third of the population is under 15 years of age, suggesting that the rate of natural increase (RNI) will not drop soon. Infant mortality continues to be high, the health of many Nicaraguans is poor, and life expectancy is one of the shortest in all of Latin America. All that can be said in a positive sense is that conditions are better today than they have been in the past. Hopefully, they will continue to improve. The keys to solving most population-related problems are good government, a robust economy, and improvements to the standard of living. There are signs that these conditions may be gaining a foothold.

Nicaraguan culture is undergoing rapid change. The country, like many other developing lands, is making the transition from a dominantly rural, traditional, self-sufficient folk culture to a contemporary urban society. As this occurs,

A worker of the Electoral Supreme Council carries ballot boxes in Managua for the November 2006 elections. Hundreds of observers from several international groups monitored the elections to make certain they were peaceful and fair.

more people become formally educated. Literacy rates have already improved, particularly in Managua, which was recently applauded throughout Central America for having eliminated illiteracy. Urban people take jobs in the manufacturing or service sector of the economy, thereby raising their incomes and standard of living.

The country is somewhat unique in that a surprisingly high percentage of the population is Protestant. This trend may continue. As tourism and globalization increase, it is also probable that more and more Nicaraguans will speak English as a second language. This is particularly true of the young, who are also encouraged to learn English because of the Internet, international sports, the media, and other elements of contemporary popular culture.

Good government is the very foundation of any successful country and economy. It is here that Nicaragua has failed throughout most of its history. The country's political track record is absolutely dismal. It may or may not bode well for the future that the president, Daniel Ortega, is a former Sandinista leader. Nonetheless, for the past two decades, Nicaragua's political landscape has been fairly calm and stable. Here, it is helpful to adopt a historical perspective. Not too many decades ago, most of Latin America, including Nicaragua, was ruled by dictators or military-controlled governments. Today, most of the region, including Nicaragua, is relatively politically stable. Nicaraguans, it is hoped, recognize that much is at stake, including their future well-being.

The Nicaraguan economy has only one way to go: up. You will recall that by many measures, only Haiti is poorer than Nicaragua among Western Hemisphere countries. After decades of civil conflict, Nicaragua's economy was in shambles. Farms and factories were destroyed, transportation and communication infrastructure was in ruins, and lawlessness prevailed. No one, whether Nicaraguan or foreign, would invest capital in the country under such hopeless conditions. After two decades of relative calm, there are signs that the economy is beginning to grow. For the most part, agricultural production has stabilized. Factories are again manufacturing products for domestic use and export. Transportation and communication linkages have been restored. Energy production and distribution has improved, and tourism is booming.

Three areas, in particular, offer hope for the future. The first is an increase in capital resources—money and the means by which money can be made. There are signs that investors are beginning to show greater confidence in the country. As this happens, more money becomes available for economic development. An increase in capital resources is essential if overall economic growth is to occur.

Second, hopes are high that recoverable oil and natural gas deposits will be found in the country's Caribbean and Pacific coastal zones. This would ease the country's chronic energy shortage and go far to help balance its import-export trade imbalance. Other energy-related developments are currently underway, including additional hydroelectric, geothermal, wind, and biomass (ethanol) installations.

A third and perhaps most important area of further economic development is the country's tourism potential. Tourists are drawn to areas that have something special to offer. Some seek historical sites and things of cultural interest. Nicaragua offers plenty of both. Others are interested in scenery and outdoor activities. Here Nicaragua is also at an advantage: The country faces upon two oceans and has two large lakes. Tourists searching for water-related activities therefore have many choices. Nicaragua's many mountains, dense forests, and varied waterscapes offer visitors a variety of scenic natural options. Some visitors seek nature in the raw, and Nicaragua can provide them with the adventures they seek.

Most tourists, however, want a well-developed tourist infrastructure that provides comfort and convenience. They want and expect such services as adequate lodging, a variety of clean restaurants, and accessible transportation, including rental vehicles. Many locations throughout the country already have these facilities. In others, they are being developed. In addition, all tourists want to know that they will be safe and secure. Today, Nicaragua boasts one of the lowest crime rates in the Western Hemisphere. Tourism is growing rapidly, and almost certainly this trend will continue.

Finally, changes may come to some of Nicaragua's regions. About half of the country remains quite remote, sparsely settled, and little is developed. Vast areas of the east and southeast cannot be reached by road. Much of the problem appears to be historical and cultural in nature. The early Spanish settlers simply avoided the Eastern Lowlands. Therefore, the country grew in the west while ignoring the east. Whereas the natural environment of the Eastern Lowlands does offer a number of challenges, it also offers opportunities. In neighboring Costa Rica, for example, the rain forest has been turned into an eco-tourist's paradise. Perhaps Nicaragua could do the same. After all, it has the largest rain forest north of the Brazilian Amazon. Many countries have developed tourist destinations along their Caribbean coastlines. Nicaragua, however, has barely tapped this potential.

Are you ready to visit Nicaragua? It is hoped that you have found it to be a fascinating country with much to offer. Oh, and if you do visit and decide to go for a swim to cool off in the sweltering tropical climate, remember the freshwater sharks!

Facts at a Glance

Note: All data 2009 unless otherwise indicated

Physical Geography

Location North America; Central American portion of Middle America, located between the Caribbean Sea (Atlantic Ocean) and North Pacific Ocean, and bordered by Honduras and Costa Rica

Area 50,336 square miles (130,370 sq km), slightly smaller than New York State

Boundaries Honduras, 573 miles (922 km); Costa Rica, 192 miles (309 km); coastal, 565 miles (910 km)

Coastline 565 miles (910 km)

Climate Wet tropical on Caribbean side; cooler temperatures in interior highlands; seasonal wet-and-dry tropical on Pacific side; precipitation varies from 250 inches (6,500 mm) in the Eastern Lowlands to 40 inches (1,000 mm) on western mountain slopes and portions of the rift valley

Terrain Extensive Atlantic coastal plains rising to central interior mountains; narrow Pacific coastal plain interrupted by volcanoes

Elevation Extremes Lowest point: Pacific Ocean, 0 feet (0 m); Highest point: Mogoton, 6,909 feet (2,107 m)

Land Use Land suited to agriculture: 15%; land permanently farmed: 2%; other: 83%

Irrigated Land 235 square miles (610 sq km) (2003)

Natural Hazards Earthquakes, volcanic eruptions, hurricanes from June through October, floods, droughts, landslides

Natural Resources Gold, silver, copper, tungsten, lead, zinc, timber, fish

Environmental Issues Soil erosion; deforestation; water pollution

People

Population 5,891,199

Population Growth Rate 1.8% per year

Net Migration Rate Net loss of 1 per 1,000 per year

Population Density 114 per square mile (44 per sq km)

Total Fertility Rate 2.57 children/woman (2.1 is replacement rate)

Birth Rate 23.25 births/1,000 population

Death Rate 4.3 deaths/1,000 population

Life Expectancy at Birth Total population: 71.5 years (male 69.4 years; female 73.8 years)

Median Age	Total: 22.1 years; male 21.7 years; female 22.5 years
Age Structure	0–14 years: 33.8%
	15–64 years: 62.9%
	65 years and over: 3.3%
Racial/Ethnic Groups	Mestizo (mixed Amerindian and white) 69%, white 17%, black 9%, Amerindian 5%
Religions	Roman Catholic 58.5%, Evangelical 21.6%, Moravian 1.6%, Jehovah's Witness 0.9%, other 1.7%, none 15.7%
Languages	Spanish 97.5% (official), Miskito 1.7%, other 0.8%
Literacy	(Age 15 and over who can read and write) Total population: 67.5%; male 67.2%; female 67.8% (2003)
Human Development Index	120 among the world's 177 ranked countries (second lowest in the Americas ahead of Haiti and tied with Guatemala)

Economy (2008)

Currency	Cordobas
GDP Purchasing Power Parity (PPP)	$16.8 billion
GDP Per Capita	$2,900
Labor Force	2.3 million
Unemployment Rate	5.6% (rate of underemployment, 46%)
Labor Force by Occupation	Agriculture 17%, industry 26%, services 57% (2006)
Population Below Poverty Line	48%
Agricultural Products	Coffee, bananas, sugarcane, cotton, rice, corn, tobacco, sesame, soya, beans; beef, veal, pork, poultry, dairy products; shrimp, lobsters
Industries	Food processing, chemicals, machinery and metal products, textiles, clothing, petroleum refining and distribution, beverages, footwear, wood
Exports	$2.92 billion
Export Commodities	Coffee, beef, shrimp and lobster, tobacco, sugar, gold, peanuts
Imports	$5.04 billion ($2.12 billion trade deficit)
Import Commodities	Consumer goods, machinery and equipment, raw materials, petroleum products
Leading Trade Partners	Exports: U.S. 32.3%, El Salvador 14.6%, Costa Rica 6.9%, Honduras 6.8%, Mexico 5.3%, Canada 5%, Guatemala 5%. Imports: U.S. 21%, Venezuela

14.3%, Mexico 8.4%, Costa Rica 8%, China 7.8%,
Guatemala 6.1%, El Salvador 5.2% (2008)

Transportation Roadways: 11,828 miles (19,036 km); 1,429 miles
(2,299 km) are paved; railways: none; airports: 144 (11
with paved runways); waterways: 1,379 miles (2,220
km); seaports: Bluefields, Corinto, El Bluff

Government

Country Name Conventional long form: Republic of Nicaragua;
conventional short form: Nicaragua; local long form:
Republica de Nicaragua; local short form: Nicaragua

Capital Managua

Type of Government Republic

Head of Government President Daniel Ortega Saavedra (since January 10,
2007)

Independence September 15, 1821 (from Spain)

Administrative Divisions 15 departments and 2 autonomous regions*; Atlantico
Norte*, Atlantico Sur*, Boaco, Carazo, Chinandega,
Chontales, Esteli, Granada, Jinotega, León, Madriz,
Managua, Masaya, Matagalpa, Nueva Segovia, Rio San
Juan, Rivas

Constitution Current constitution adopted January 9, 1987; revised in
1995, 2000, and 2005

Communications

TV Stations 3 (1997)

Radio Stations 96 (AM: 63; FM: 32; shortwave: 1) (1998)

Phones 312,000 mainline telephones (2008); 3 million cellular
phones (2008)

Internet Users 88,742 Internet hosts (2009); 185,000 Internet users
(2008)

B.C.

Before 20,000 Possible human presence in Central America

A.D.

1502 Christopher Columbus lands on Nicaraguan coast.

1522 Spanish explorers reach Lake Nicaragua; cities of Grenada and León founded; Spaniards name Nicaragua for Nicarao, a local tribal chief.

1524 Francisco Hernández de Córdoba completes conquest of Nicaragua for Spain.

1529 War of the Captains.

1687 British claim Caribbean Miskito Coast.

1821 Nicaragua declares independence from Spain and joins Mexican Empire.

1823 Nicaragua becomes part of the United Provinces of Central America.

1838 Nicaragua achieves full independence as a republic.

1870s Coffee becomes chief Nicaraguan agricultural crop.

1894 Nicaragua regains control of Miskito Coast.

1911 United States begins period of military and financial intervention that lasts until 1933.

1932 Managua destroyed by earthquake.

1933 U.S. Marines leave Nicaragua.

1937 General Anastasio Somoza Garcia becomes president; Somoza family holds power for more than four decades.

1956 Somoza assassinated; sons Luis and Anastasio, Jr., retain control of government.

1972 Earthquake devastates Managua, killing more than 5,000 and leaving more than 250,000 homeless.

1979 Sandinistas overthrow government and President Anastasio Somoza Debayle flees the country.

1981 United States suspends aid to Nicaragua and gives support to "freedom fighters" called Contras.

1984 Sandinista leader Daniel Ortega is elected president.

1988 Hurricane Joan leaves 180,000 people homeless.

1990 Violeta Chamorro, wife of assassinated politician Pedro Joaquín Chamorro, defeats Ortega in presidential election; Sandinistas and the Contras sign a permanent cease-fire and the Contras demobilize.

1998 Hurricane Mitch causes severe flooding and extensive damage to infrastructure and property and kills an estimated 10,000 Nicaraguans.

2001 Nicaragua experiences severe economic crisis due to a prolonged drought and sharp decline in coffee prices.

2005 Central America Free Trade Agreement (CAFTA) with the United States is implemented after several years of negotiations.

2006 Daniel Ortega wins presidential election and returns to office in 2007.

Bermann, Karl. *Under the Big Stick: Nicaragua and the United States Since 1848.* Boston: South End Press, 1986.

Bugajski, Janusz. *Sandinista Communism and Rural Nicaragua.* (The Washington Papers, 143.) New York: Praeger, 1990.

Espinosa Estrada, Jorge. *Nicaragua, Cuna de America* (*Nicaragua, Cradle of "America"*). Managua, 1969.

Gilbert, Dennis. *Sandinistas: The Party and the Revolution.* Cambridge, Mass.: B. Blackwell, 1990.

Gritzner, Charles F. "Chickens, Worms, and a Little Bull: Some Animated Perspectives on American History." *Journal of Geography* 76, no. 5 (March 1977): 111–112.

Marcou, Jules. *Atlantic Monthly* 35 (1875): 291–296.

———. "Amerique, Amerigho Vespucci, and America." *Annual Report of the Board of Regents of the Smithsonian Institution,* 1890.

Morley, Morris H. *Washington, Somoza, and the Sandinistas: State and Regime in U.S. Policy Toward Nicaragua, 1969–1981.* Cambridge, England: Cambridge University Press, 1994.

Nietschmann, B. *Between Land and Water: The Subsistence Ecology of the Miskito Indians, Eastern Nicaragua.* New York: Seminar Press, 1973.

Sabia, Debra. *Contradiction and Conflict: The Popular Church in Nicaragua.* Tuscaloosa: University of Alabama Press, 1997.

Sauer, Carl Ortwin. *The Early Spanish Main.* Berkeley and Los Angeles: University of California Press, 1966/1992.

Walker, Thomas W. *Nicaragua, the Land of Sandino.* (Nations of Contemporary Latin America.) Boulder, Colo.: Westview Press, 1981.

West, Robert Cooper, and John P. Augelli. *Middle America: Its Lands and Peoples.* Englewood, N.J.: Prentice-Hall, 1966/1989.

Further Reading

Dall, Christopher. *Nicaragua in Pictures.* Minneapolis, Minn.: Twenty-first Century Books, 2007.

Kott, Jennifer, and Kristi Streiffert. *Nicaragua.* (Cultures of the World.) New York: Marshall Cavendish Benchmark, 2005.

Morrison, Marion. *Nicaragua.* New York: Children's Press, 2002.

Shields, Charles J. *Nicaragua.* (Central America Today.) Broomall, Penn.: Mason Crest Publishers, 2009.

White, Randy Wayne. *The Sharks of Lake Nicaragua: True Tales of Adventure, Travel, and Fishing.* New York: Lyon's Press, 2000.

White, Steven F., and Esthela Calderón. *Culture and Customs of Nicaragua.* Westport, Conn.: Greenwood Press, 2008.

Web sites

Encyclopedia.com
http://www.encyclopedia.com/doc/1G2-2586700166.html

Frommer's
http://www.frommers.com/destinations/nicaragua/

Lonely Planet
http://www.lonelyplanet.com/nicaragua

NationMaster.com
http://www.nationmaster.com/countries

New World Encyclopedia
http://www.newworldencyclopedia.org/entry/Nicaragua

U.S. Department of State: Background Notes
http://www.state.gov/r/pa/ei/bgn/1850.htm

U.S. Library of Congress
http://rs6.loc.gov/frd/cs/nitoc.html

U.S. State Department Bureau of Counselor Affairs
http://travel.state.gov/travel/cis_pa_tw/cis/cis_985.html

ViaNica.com: Foods
http://www.vianica.com/go/specials/2-nicaraguan_food.html

ViaNica.com: Volcanoes
http://www.vianica.com/go/specials/9-nicaragua-volcanoes.html

Wikipedia: Human Development Index
http://en.wikipedia.org/wiki/List_of_countries_by_Human_Development_Index

Wikitravel: Nicaragua
http://wikitravel.org/en/Nicaragua

Picture Credits

Index

Index

About the Author

Series editor **CHARLES F. GRITZNER** is Distinguished Professor of Geography Emeritus at South Dakota State University. He retired after 50 years of college teaching and now looks forward to what he hopes to be many more years of research and writing. Gritzner has served as both president and executive director of the National Council for Geographic Education and has received the council's highest honor, the George J. Miller Award for Distinguished Service to Geographic Education, as well as other honors from the NCGE, the Association of American Geographers, and other organizations.